the
civil war
within

biblical "facts of life" in the struggle for spiritual growth

wayne taylor

The Civil War Within
Biblical "Facts of Life" in the Struggle for Spiritual Growth

Copyright © 2004 by Wayne Taylor

Published by Calvary Fellowship
23302 - 56th Ave. West
Mountlake Terrace, WA 98043

© Wayne Taylor 1989
Revised 1994
Reprinted 2004
Revision Editors: Jeff & Jan Nelson

1-931667-84-5

Printed in the United States

I would like to rededicate this new, updated book to the funniest family on earth—*my family*:

My ever-faithful mom, Betty

My beautiful, talented daughter, Amy

My firstborn, big-hearted son, Jordan

My creative, musical, artist-boy, Riley

My sensitive, amusing, scholar-child, Nick

And most of all, my eternally youthful, smart, and gorgeous wife, Cathy

contents

foreword

Paul the apostle declared in his letter to the Ephesians that the purpose of gifted men in the church was to bring the believers into a spiritual maturity in Christ, so that they would no longer be as babes that were tossed to and fro with every wind of doctrine.

One of the greatest needs for the believer in Jesus Christ is to come into spiritual maturity. The book of Romans, chapters one through eight, is designed by the Spirit to bring you to maturity, yet so few Christians ever make that trek all of the way. We, like the children of Israel, seem to get stalled in the wilderness. For years, I was in an arrested state of spiritual development, which had existed even through the first seven years of my being in the ministry. If it were not for the work of the Spirit in opening up the book of Romans to my heart, I might still be there. But God through His grace and truth brought me from a life of spiritual defeat into the beautiful life of victory and rest in Jesus.

In this book, Wayne Taylor uses his God-given gifts of pastor-teacher to expound the truths of Romans so as to lead you along the path from infancy to a full maturity in Christ. A careful reading of this book will revolutionize your

Christian walk and bring you into the fullness of joy that should mark your relationship with Jesus.

Chuck Smith
Pastor, Calvary Chapel Costa Mesa

introduction

I decided to subtitle this book "Facts of Life" because it is especially for Christians who are in what I call "spiritual puberty." They are in a strange and awkward time in their Christian walk because they are in a transition to something greater.

When I was twelve or thirteen years old, I went through a time of emotional and physical change. My mom tried to get my dad to tell me about the facts of life: the birds and the bees. My dad refused to do it, so my mom got me a book … the infamous "book." I'm glad she did, because as I read, I began to understand more about myself. For one thing, I was going through great physical changes. My voice was changing from a soprano to a tenor, little bumps were breaking out on my face, and other physical changes were taking place. Emotionally, I was beginning to be very attracted to the opposite sex. I was also becoming very disgusted with my parents—I thought they knew nothing.

To sum it up, while I was in the throes of the "junior high puberty blues," reading through that book helped me understand a little bit more about myself.

Many Christians feel they are in "spiritual adolescence." Emotionally and spiritually, they find themselves in a no-man's land—feeling like they need to change, but not knowing how.

There are spiritual facts about God contained in His Word that can launch you into a healthy growth and fruitfulness in Jesus Christ. All true spiritual growth comes from knowing the principles of God's Word. Jesus said to His disciples:

> If you abide in My word, you are My disciples indeed. And you shall know the truth, and the truth shall make you free.
>
> *John 8:31–32, NKJV*

If you take these principles to heart, it will free you to enjoy genuine growth and fruitfulness in your walk with Christ.

1

prologue: civil war

Civil war is the worst kind of conflict a nation can go through—much worse than being attacked by an outside aggressor. The horrible civil wars in Bosnia and Lebanon are modern examples. Those people literally destroyed themselves and their countries.

At any given time, every born-again Christian has either the potential or the reality of a fierce inner civil war occurring. The Bible says in Galatians 5:17:

> For the flesh sets its desire against the Spirit, and the Spirit against the flesh; for these are in opposition to one another, so that you may not do the things that you please.

This hostility within ourselves is even worse than the struggle we have with the devil or with this hostile world in which we live. It is truly a civil war—an inner battle between ourselves—the old and the new, the flesh and the spirit. Every Christian, including the most zealous, struggles with this terrible conflict of natures.

Samuel Rutherford said, "Every man blameth the devil

for his sins; but the great devil, the house-devil of every man, the house-devil that eateth and lieth in every man's bosom, is that idol that killeth all, himself."[1]

sin remains

Hudson Taylor, the pioneering missionary to China who was greatly used by God, found himself caught in this conflict. He wrote:

> I felt the ingratitude, the danger, the sin of not living nearer to God. I prayed, agonized, fasted, strove, made resolutions, read the Word more diligently, sought more time for meditation—but all without avail. Every day, almost every hour, the consciousness of sin oppressed me.
>
> I knew that if only I could abide in Christ all would be well, but I could not. I would begin the day with prayer, determined not to take my eye off Him for a moment, but pressure of duties, sometimes very trying, and constant interruptions apt to be so wearing, caused me to forget Him. Then one's nerves get so fretted in this climate that temptations to irritability, hard thoughts, and sometimes unkind words are all the more difficult to control. Each day brought its register of sin and failure, but lack of power. To will was indeed "present with me," but how to perform I found not.[2]

freedom

One of the positive results of the American Civil War, horrible as it was, was the emancipation of the slaves. Just as they eventually experienced the benefits of freedom, it is God's will for us to learn to win that great inner civil war. The Lord wants to emancipate us from all that enslaves us, not only from sin, but also from legalism, self, and the flesh. He wants to bring us into fullness with Jesus Christ.

For us to enter into that fullness, vital biblical truths must be carefully laid as a rock-solid foundation for our Christian lives. These truths have changed the lives of some of history's greatest Christians, and have literally changed the course of history itself.

2

bad news / good news

The principles we will examine in this book have transformed millions of lives throughout history. An example is Saint Augustine. The truths found in the book of Romans brought Augustine to a place of conversion. Though this man was an intellectual, he was overwhelmed by the wisdom of God.

Martin Luther was a Roman Catholic priest who had a very frustrating relationship with the Lord. As he began to read these basic truths in the book of Romans, God took hold of him. Luther explained, "I greatly longed to understand Paul's epistle to the Romans, and nothing stood in the way but that one expression, 'the justice of God,' because I took it to mean that justice whereby God is just and deals justly in punishing the unjust. My situation was that, although an impeccable monk, I stood before God as a sinner troubled in conscience, and I had no confidence that my merit would assuage Him. Therefore I didn't love a just and angry God, but I rather hated and murmured against Him. Yet I clung to the dear Paul and had a great longing to learn what he meant. Night and day I pondered until I saw the connection between the justice of God and the statement that 'the just shall live by his faith.'

"Then I grasped that the justice of God is that righteousness by which through grace and sheer mercy God justifies us through faith. Thereupon I felt myself to have been reborn and to have gone through open doors into paradise. The whole of Scripture took on new meaning, and whereas before the justice of God had filled me with hate, now it became to me inexpressible sweet and greater love. This passage of Paul became to me a gate to heaven."[3]

John Wesley, another example of a person whose life was affected by these principles, helped bring about the great evangelical revival of the eighteenth century. The same was true of Charles Spurgeon in the early nineteenth century and D.L. Moody in the early twentieth century.

More recently, Pastor Chuck Smith of Calvary Chapel in Costa Mesa, California, and others have understood these principles of God's grace so clearly taught in His Word. They are the human instruments who brought about the "Jesus Movement" of the late 1960s and early 1970s. Many of today's Christians are the fruit of that movement. All of these great movements of God were spawned by the "facts of life" we will examine in this book.

we need Jesus

We begin by looking at both the bad news and the good news of the gospel. When I first became a Christian, my salvation didn't mean that much to me because I didn't comprehend how bad I really was. When God began to show me my true self, my life was transformed. As we begin our study, I trust that God will reveal to you how bad you are. Though this doesn't sound like a nice revelation, the benefits will be life changing.

Mankind's problem is that we are totally sinful, completely selfish, and incapable of any purely good thing. In the sight of God, we are hopeless, helpless sinners. Few of us realize this when we first come to Jesus Christ. We acknowledge we are sinners, thank God for our salvation and go on with our lives. After a while, the Lord begins to show us our true selves, which causes us to think we need to be saved all over again. This is because most Christians don't comprehend the totality of their sinfulness. Because we don't realize how sinful we are, we don't readily or fully appreciate God's salvation and His gift of righteousness.

The first "fact of life" we need to understand is the bad news: We are sinful and have no capacity to please God in our own strength. We won't completely experience the benefits of our salvation until we understand our sinful nature. By recognizing our total need as sinners, we will be driven to a total dependency on Jesus. Until we recognize this, we won't enter into all that Jesus offers us; nor are we going to love Jesus Christ as much as we would if we realized how desperately we need Him.

the gospel

Paul wrote to the church at Rome, "For I am not ashamed of the gospel of Christ, for it is the power of God to salvation for everyone who believes, for the Jew first and also for the

Greek. For in it the righteousness of God is revealed from faith to faith; as it is written, 'The just shall live by faith' " (Romans 1:16–17, NKJV).

These two verses sum up the main theme of the book of Romans: the gospel of Jesus Christ. In the remainder of the book, Paul goes on to explain and elaborate on this main theme.

Paul starts out in Romans by giving his readers the bad news. The first eight chapters of Romans are a systematic, beautiful, spiritual work of art laying out all the glory of the gospel of Jesus. Like a skilled artist, Paul starts by painting a black background. For the first two and a half chapters, he presents the utter and absolute sinful nature of mankind.

the decline of mankind

In the first chapter of Romans, we have a description of the decline of mankind. Step by step, Paul describes our terrible decline into sin. It begins very subtly and simply.

Paul writes, "Since the creation of the world His invisible attributes, His eternal power and divine nature, have been clearly seen, being understood through what has been made, …" (1:20a). In other words, through the physical creation we find evidence for God's existence. Hence, "… they are without excuse" (1:20b). This is the first step down. "For even though they knew God, they did not honor Him as God or give thanks; but they became futile in their speculations" (1:21).

the civil war within

step one: unwillingness to worship

The first step down is an unwillingness to worship our Creator. Because creation testifies of the reality of God, there is not a person alive who has an excuse. Our conscience also testifies of the reality of God. For these reasons, it is inexcusable for us to refuse to worship and glorify the Creator.

step two: blocking God from our mind

Paul then gives a second downward step, "And just as they did not see fit to acknowledge God any longer ..." (1:28a). This literally means "they did not see fit to have God in their knowledge any longer." The second step down is pushing God out of our knowledge. It is troublesome when we want to sin and the knowledge of God is in our minds. When we are thinking about God and have knowledge of Him, it has an influence of turning us away from sin and curbing our sinful desires. When the knowledge of God is in our minds, it is difficult to sin. If we want to sin, we must temporarily block the knowledge of God out of our minds while we indulge in that sin.

step three: useless thoughts

Paul continues giving us the steps down, "They became futile in their speculations, and their foolish heart was darkened. Professing to be wise, they became fools" (Romans 1:21,22). If you are unwilling to worship God and you block Him out of your mind, something will fill your thoughts. These new thoughts will be empty, vain, and foolish. The Bible says, "The fool has said in his heart, 'There is no God' " (Psalm 14:1). They have refused to worship God and have blocked Him out of their minds.

step four: idolatry

"[They] exchanged the glory of the incorruptible God for an image in the form of corruptible man ... they exchanged the truth of God for a lie, and worshiped and served the creature rather than the Creator" (Romans 1:23,25). The fourth step down is idolatry—idolizing things created instead of the Creator. You can idolize any number of things; it might be a person, home, your car, your intellect, or your pleasures.

step five: sexual immorality

The fifth step down is sexual immorality. "Therefore God gave them over in the lusts of their hearts to impurity, so that their bodies would be dishonored among them" (Romans 1: 24). Sexual immorality, including homosexuality, which is described in this chapter as "unnatural," is a result of the failure to worship God.

Once a person refuses to worship God and blocks Him out of their mind, it opens the door to all manner of evil. God then gives the result:

Just as they did not see fit to acknowledge God any longer, God gave them over to a depraved mind, to do those things which are not proper, being filled

9

with all unrighteousness, wickedness, greed, evil;
full of envy, murder, strife, deceit, malice; they are
gossips, slanderers, haters of God, insolent, arrogant,
boastful, inventors of evil, disobedient to parents,
without understanding, untrustworthy, unloving,
unmerciful; and although they know the ordinance of
God, that those who practice such things are worthy of
death, they not only do the same, but also give hearty
approval to those who practice them.

Romans 1:28–32

This is the decline of man.

i'm not that bad

Now, if you are thinking that you aren't like those horrible
people, consider what Paul says next:

Therefore you have no excuse, everyone of you who
passes judgment, for in that which you judge another,
you condemn yourself; for you who judge practice the
same things. And we know that the judgment of God
rightly falls upon those who practice such things. But
do you suppose this, O man, when you pass judgment
on those who practice such things and do the same
yourself, that you will escape the judgment of God?

Romans 2:1–3

Even Christians have this funny idea that we aren't so
bad. The Bible, however, says we are. We object, "I'm not as
bad as him," or, "I'm not as bad as her, or that drunk, or that

addict." The Lord made it apparent to me after eight or nine years of walking with Him that I was worse than any sinner I'd ever met or seen in my life. He began to show me the fact that in my heart I did the very things I condemned in other people. This is because my heart is wicked, it is "deceitful above all things, and desperately wicked" (Jeremiah 17:9, NKJV). He began to show me my inner self and I didn't like what I saw.

Isaiah the prophet wrote:

Then you will call, and the LORD will answer; you will cry, and He will say, "Here I am." If you remove the yoke from your midst, *the pointing of the finger* and speaking wickedness … then your light will rise in darkness.

Isaiah 58:9–10, italics added

The British preacher, Roy Hession, commented on this Scripture:

When you point the finger at someone else, not only are there three fingers pointing back at you, but there is also your thumb pointing up at God. That sort of thing leads to the clenched fist. Spiritual revival is the finger of God pointing at me.

Second, it is the finger of the Spirit pointing at Christ on your behalf. That is revival. Revival is the finger of God pointing at you first, then it is the finger of the Spirit pointing at Christ.[4]

11

Hession also observes that this sort of action leads to the open hand ready to receive. Put away the pointing of the finger, then you will call and God will answer.

Chapter 2 of Romans is especially directed at those who see themselves as very moral and spiritual. The first chapter of Romans is written to the ordinary sinner, while the second chapter is for the Jews, and for those who have moral, religious and spiritual training; those who would self-righteously justify themselves and condemn others. Genuine Christianity never leads you to self-righteousness or judgmentalism. Never. Why? Because you realize you are just as wicked and guilty as anyone else and your salvation and righteousness is a wonderful gift from God. True Christianity leads to the utmost humility, compassion, mercy, and zealous, godly love.

Therefore, in the first chapter of Romans, Paul speaks of "they" and "them," but in Romans chapter 2, he speaks of "you." He writes, "Therefore *you* are without excuse, every man of *you* who passes judgment" (Romans 2:1, NASB, italics added); and then in verse 5, "But because of *your* stubbornness and unrepentant heart you are storing up wrath for yourself in the day of wrath and revelation of the righteous judgment of God" (italics added).

God's indictment of us

As Paul goes into Romans chapter 3, he talks about "we" and "us," and gives his final argument. When lawyers are arguing their case, at the end of the trial they give their summarizing statements to the jury. This is Paul's statement: "What then? Are we better than they? Not at all; for we have already charged that both Jews and Greeks are all under sin" (Romans 3:9). Paul then states, "As it is written," and goes on in the next nine verses to cite nine passages from the Old Testament to solidify his case—giving God's indictment of the human race. Notice the all-inclusive words here, "As it is written, 'There is *none* righteous, *not even one*; there is *none* who understands, there is *none* who seeks for God; all have turned aside, together they have become useless; there is *none* who does good, there is *not even one*' " (Romans 3:10–12, italics added). That covers it.

Referring to anyone who doesn't have a relationship with God, Paul goes on to say, "Their throat is an open grave, with their tongues they keep deceiving, the poison of asps is under their lips" (Romans 3:13). It is as though God, the Great Physician, is giving mankind a check-up. He says, "Open your mouth," then looks down our throats and gives the general state of our well-being. As God looks down our spiritual and moral throats into our hearts, He says we are an open grave. The Lord wants to get to the source of our sickness. We aren't going to enter in and experience the fullness of what He has if we are still looking to the source of self. He wants to point out just how bad it is so we will flee to Him and enter fully into what He has made available.

helpless and ungodly

In Romans chapter 5, Paul carefully chooses four words to

describe our condition. The first two words are *helpless* and *ungodly*. In verse 6, he says, "For while we were still helpless, at the right time Christ died for the ungodly." *Helpless* literally means "strengthless." We have absolutely no spiritual or moral power within us with which to save ourselves from our moral corruption. There would be more hope for a dog to become human than for us to be acceptable to God.

There are some people who like to dress up their dogs. I once had a neighbor who was an older lady and a bit eccentric. She didn't have any children, just her little doggie. It was a small poodle, and she would put a sweater on it, along with little booties and a hat. But when she took her dressed-up doggie for a walk, it would still walk through the mud and go over to the fire hydrant. It was a dog. You can dress it up, but it will remain a dog.

The same is true of us. We can try to dress ourselves up with a little bit of religion, but it won't do. Trying to be good won't do either. That is why man-made religion, philosophy, and humanism are absolutely powerless as far as saving us from our corruption. It just rearranges our sinfulness and "dresses it up" a little. You can become a sophisticated sinner, but that is all you can become apart from Christ. The word "ungodly" literally means "no reverence or respect for God."

The third word in Romans chapter 5 that describes our condition is *sinners*. Verse 8 says, "God demonstrates His own love toward us, in that while we were yet sinners. …" Paul is saying we are "offenders of God, rejecters of God's authority." The fourth word, *enemies*, is used in verse 10 and means "to hate." People are angry at God and hate His control.

The conclusion concerning our condition is found in God's Law:

> Now we know that whatever the Law says, it speaks to those who are under the Law, so that every mouth may be closed and all the world may become accountable to God; because by the works of the Law no flesh will be justified in His sight; for through the Law comes the knowledge of sin.

> *Romans 3:19–20*

God's standard is in His Law and it shows us four truths. First, at the end of verse 20, the Law shows us our sinfulness. God's standard was given to bring to us the knowledge of sin. Second, the Law shows us that no one can be justified by trying to live up to God's standard because we all fail (v. 20). Then in verse 19, God's standard and Law also show us that we are all accountable to Him.

letting God justify you

Finally, God's Law shows us that "every mouth may be closed" (v. 19). God's standard tells us to shut up, to quit excusing ourselves, and to quit blaming others as if they are at fault for our problems. *They* aren't at fault, *we* are! Do you justify your wrong behavior? Do you defend yourself? While we keep defending and excusing ourselves, God is saying, "Shut up." As long as we keep justifying ourselves, we won't enter into that justification He has provided for us and we won't experience the glory of His righteousness.

The next time you are in an argument and you feel a great need to justify yourself, why don't you just shut up? Point your finger at yourself for a while and see if the Lord has answers for you. His finger is pointing at you, but His finger will also point to Christ.

Paul has described how horrible we are for one purpose—not to make us feel bad, but so we can get to the good news. You need to realize who you are, how lost you are apart from Christ, and that without Him there is no hope. Once you have realized that, you can understand Romans 3: 21–24:

> Now apart from the Law the righteousness of God has been manifested, being witnessed by the Law and the Prophets, even the righteousness of God through faith in Jesus Christ for all those who believe; for there is no distinction; for all have sinned and fall short of the glory of God, being justified as a gift by His grace [His free, unmerited favor] through the redemption which is in Christ Jesus.

Paul paints a black picture so that we will quit justifying ourselves, and instead let God justify us through simple, humble faith in His Son.

Eight years after I became a Christian, I realized how badly I needed all that was available to me in Christ. God painted that black picture so He could come to us and say, "Here is your total, complete, eternal righteousness." The only righteousness there is with God is righteousness by faith, totally apart from the Law or our own attempts at working to be good enough. Whether it be the Old Testament Law or any man-made system of law, we can't save ourselves.

Paul said, "I am not ashamed of the gospel, … For in it the righteousness of God is revealed from faith to faith; as it is written, 'But the righteous man shall live by faith' " (Romans 1:16–17). Righteous people become righteous by the faith given to them as a gift. It is all of Christ, nothing of us. Once you believe and enter in more and more fully, His gift of righteousness starts working for you, rather than you working to be righteous. We won't experience this as long as we are still trying to justify ourselves.

forgiven much, love much

Luke chapter 7 records the story of a Pharisee who invited Jesus into his home. There was also an immoral woman who entered the house. While Jesus was reclining at the table, this woman brought in a vial of perfume. She stood at His feet weeping and began to wet His feet with her tears. She then wiped His feet with her hair, and kissed His feet and anointed them with the perfume. Verse 39 says, "When the Pharisee who had invited Him saw this, he said to himself, 'If this man were a prophet He would know who and what sort of person this woman is who is touching Him, that she is a sinner.' "

So Jesus told him a story.

"A certain moneylender had two debtors: one owed five hundred denarii, and the other fifty. When they were unable to repay, he graciously forgave them both. Which of them therefore will love him more?"

Simon answered and said, "I suppose the one whom he forgave more." And He said to him, "You have judged correctly."

And turning toward the woman, He said to Simon, "Do you see this woman? I entered your house; you gave Me no water for My feet, but she has wet My feet with her tears, and wiped them with her hair. You gave Me no kiss; but she, since the time I came in, has not ceased to kiss My feet. You did not anoint My head with oil, but she anointed My feet with perfume. For this reason I say to you, her sins, which are many, have been forgiven, for she loved much; but he who is forgiven little, loves little." And He said to her, "Your sins have been forgiven."

Luke 7:40–48, NASB

Do you love Jesus to the point that you would wipe His feet with your tears of joy and appreciation, to the point that you would kiss His feet? Are you passionately in love with Him because of what He has done for you? You should be. You are depraved without Him. The beauty of recognizing your sinfulness is that you can then begin enjoying Jesus' forgiveness and His gift of total righteousness. As a result, your love for Him will be overwhelming and will result in tremendous benefits.

So, the first "fact of life" is the bad news: You are a wretch. But then there's the good news: If you put your faith in Christ, you are totally and absolutely righteous.

3

Jesus Christ— the believer's standing and source

I live in Seattle, Washington, which is located next to a body of water called Puget Sound. To cross the Sound, people most often travel on a ferryboat. Let's suppose that there were two men who wanted to cross Puget Sound from Seattle to Bremerton, but neither of them wanted to take the ferry. Perhaps they felt it took too long or was too big. For some reason, they didn't want to go across on a ferryboat. So, each one of these men determined that they were going to jump from the Seattle ferry dock to Bremerton—a distance of twenty miles.

One of the men was very sickly and uncoordinated. He ran and took the best jump he could, but unfortunately, he was only able to go three feet. He immediately sunk to the bottom and drowned. The other fellow was an imposing physical specimen with bulging muscles. He was also a world-class long-jumper and a tremendous athlete. He gathered up all his steam, ran down the ferry dock and took the longest, farthest jump he could possibly take. He managed to jump an incredible thirty-five feet, landed in Puget Sound, and drowned. The moral of the story is that the man who was able to jump the farthest drowned in the deepest water.

Some people appear to be very good and moral without God. They believe their upstanding lives should be enough for God, if indeed there is a God. If they were to ever face Him, they believe that God would accept them. These people have a hard time seeing their need for Jesus Christ because they think they are righteous in themselves. They don't realize, "There is none righteous, not even one; there is none who understands, there is none who seeks for God; all have turned aside, together they have become useless; there is none who does good, there is not even one" (Romans 3:10–12).

Those who haven't been able to see the sinful and selfish condition of their own hearts and motives aren't going to see a great need for Jesus. Unfortunately, there are also many Christians who have a problem seeing their need for Jesus. They haven't yet seen how selfish and lost they really are apart from Him. Too many are still relying on themselves, thinking they are just fine; looking to themselves as the source, rather than enjoying the provision God has made for them in Christ Jesus. Maybe some of us need to pray, "Lord, show me myself and my need for You." Helen McDowell expresses this need in her poem, *Once I Prayed:*

> *Once I prayed*
> *(I knew not what I said)*
> *"Show me myself, O Lord!"*
> *Alas, I did not dread*
> *The hideous sight*
> *(Which now I shudder to behold)*

Jesus Christ—the believer's standing and source

Because I knew not self aright.

And I was led
  In answer to my prayer,
As step by step, to see
  My wretched heart laid bare;
Then I prayed,
  "Stay, Lord, I cannot bear the sight!"
And pityingly His hand was stayed.

Now I pray
  (I know the prayer is right),
"Show me Thyself, O Lord,
  Be to my soul the Bright
And Morning Star
  To shine upon the grave of self,
And lead my heart from earth afar!"[5]

God's standard of righteousness is perfect justice, perfect righteousness, and perfect love. No one except Jesus Christ has lived up to that standard, and God isn't going to lower His standard. He has never lowered it in the past, and He won't lower it now in order that some people can be accepted.

Many people believe that God is grading on the curve. They assume that they are just as good as, or not as bad as the next person, and they think that will make them acceptable with God. Not so. I had a math teacher in the ninth grade who was impossible. He never smiled unless he was working on a math problem … This teacher did math in his spare time! His class was so difficult that unless he graded on the curve, we would have all flunked. My average was 47 percent that year, and I received a B. I had one of the higher grades (he didn't give anyone an A), but it wouldn't have looked good to flunk everybody.

God doesn't do that; He doesn't lower His standard. You may appear to be better than someone else, but God's standard is Jesus, and we all fall short of living up to that standard. In God's standard, the Bible, He tells us, "By the works of the Law no flesh will be justified in His sight; for through the Law comes the knowledge of sin" (Romans 3: 20). There is absolutely no hope for us in ourselves to be acceptable or righteous before God.

good news

Along with that gloomy introduction, God has some fantastic news for us:

> But now apart from the Law the righteousness of God has been manifested, being witnessed by the Law and the Prophets, even the righteousness of God through faith in Jesus Christ for all those who believe; for there is no distinction; for all have sinned and fall short of the glory of God, being justified as a gift by His grace through the redemption which is in Christ Jesus; whom God displayed publicly as a propitiation in His blood through faith.
>
> *Romans 3:21–25*

God has provided for us justification and righteousness in Christ through simple faith.

Let's consider the characteristics of this righteousness and acceptance with God. First, it is apart from the Law. These verses are not only referring to the Old Testament Law of God, but also to any system of works for righteousness. The righteousness of God is completely separate from doing anything to earn it, or living up to a standard to acquire it.

This is a revolutionary concept in many Christian churches, because most churches and religious systems insist on some kind of works in order to gain God's righteousness. For example, I was brought up in a church where it was very well known what you did or didn't do in order to be right with God. These do's and don'ts were listed on their Bible college application. In order to attend, I had to promise what I would and wouldn't do. If I lived up to their standards, then I would be considered righteous. I tried my best to live up to those standards of righteousness. On good days, I felt really righteous—so righteous that I had to tell people about it. On other days, I didn't do so well and I questioned if I was even a Christian. I wondered if I was right with God. Every Sunday, I was always exhorted to come down to the front and "get right with God."

This kind of "righteousness" is contrary to the righteousness of God described in Romans Chapter 3. The problem with righteousness based in law was shown in God's Old Covenant Law with Israel. Israel's problem was not with the Law of God—it is perfect. Their problem was that no one could live up to it. Paul wrote:

What the Law could not do, weak as it was through the

flesh, God did: sending His own Son in the likeness of sinful flesh and as an offering for sin.

Romans 8:3

The Law couldn't do it because, in my flesh and sinful nature, I couldn't live up to that righteous standard. Thus, this kind of righteousness is apart from the Law. The righteousness of God is not based on what *we* do for it, but it is based on what *Christ* has done for you.

in Jesus Christ

Second, Romans 3:21–25 tells us that God's righteousness, His acceptance of us, is in Jesus Christ. Notice twice: First, Romans 3:22 says, "in Jesus Christ," then verse 24 says, "The redemption which is in Christ Jesus."

Do not think the righteousness you received with God is a private possession, or that because you believe in Jesus Christ, God will give you an independent righteousness of your own. When you put your faith in Jesus Christ and receive Him, He Himself becomes your righteousness. First Corinthians 1:30 says, "By His doing you are in Christ Jesus, who became to us wisdom from God, and righteousness." As soon as you believe in Him, He becomes your righteousness. According to 2 Corinthians 5:21, "[God] made Him who knew no sin to be sin on our behalf, so that we might become the righteousness of God in Him." God sees you in the same way He sees His Son Jesus Christ because you are in Him. He causes you to be acceptable to God. You will never become more right with God than the moment you put your faith in

Jesus. From that moment, you have the same standing with God as Jesus Christ. Even though you will become more like Christ as you daily walk with Him, you will never become more right with God.

by His grace

The righteousness of God is by His grace. Paul says we have "been justified," or declared righteous "as a gift by His grace." The word translated "grace" in Greek is *charis,* from which we get the English word "charity." The only people who receive charity are those who are in desperate need. When it comes to righteousness, we are all bankrupt, because as Romans 3:23 says, "For all have sinned and fall short of the glory of God." Not only have we sinned in the past, we still fall short of the glory of God. We have no righteousness in ourselves; thus, we need charity. God, in His love and charity, has given us a gift that allows us to have a right standing with Him. It is by grace.

Later, Paul adds, "But if it is by grace, it is no longer on the basis of works, otherwise grace is no longer grace" (Romans 11:6). What you work for is not charity. Therefore, you can't mix righteousness by faith and righteousness by works. It is like oil and water; it is either one or the other.

free gift

The righteousness of God is also a free gift. The Greek word for "gift" means "for nothing." There are those who add certain works to the gospel of Jesus Christ that are required in order to gain salvation. They do this because they don't want to be accused of preaching "cheap grace." The message of Paul is that grace is a free gift that you can't do a thing to earn. That doesn't mean it came without an incredible cost in terms of a price. We need to realize what God paid: He gave everything in the person of His Son Jesus Christ, and Jesus Christ gave everything by shedding His own life's blood. Truly receiving His grace and realizing the love God has for us will produce the highest commitment and the deepest devotion.

Finally, we are declared righteous "being justified as a gift by His grace through the redemption which is in Christ Jesus" (Romans 3:24). Here we see the cost. The word "redeemed" means "to buy a slave out of bondage in order to set him free." Jesus paid the price of your redemption, buying you out of slavery to sin in order to set you free. First Peter 1, verses 18 and 19 say:

> You were not redeemed with perishable things like silver or gold from your futile way of life inherited from your forefathers, but with precious blood, as of a lamb unblemished and spotless, the blood of Christ.

through His blood

"… The redemption which is in Christ Jesus; whom God displayed publicly as a propitiation in His blood through faith" (Romans 3:24b–25a). The blood of Christ propitiated the Father for you—the redemption was through His blood. This means His blood appeased the Father's wrath toward your sin, released His mercy toward you as a sinner, and satisfied God's judgment against you. God doesn't have any more wrath to pour out on the believer because Jesus' death for us totally satisfied His wrath. As Christians, our "Judgment Day" is past in the sense of God's final punishment for our sins. That day of judgment against the believer's sins took place when Jesus died for us. Now, all God has is mercy toward the believer.

"If we confess our sins, [God] is faithful and righteous to forgive us our sins and to cleanse us from all unrighteousness" (1 John 1:9). When believers in Christ come to Him confessing their sins, it is only right for God to forgive them. Because Jesus paid the price, God forgives and declares us righteous by faith in Jesus Christ. Christ becomes our righteousness. Therefore, when our faith is in Christ Jesus, we receive complete justification.

This righteousness of God is by faith—all we can do to gain it is believe in Christ. Faith is merely the hand that receives it, not some work that you strain and strive to obtain. Faith is reaching out and saying, "Yes, I receive that, I believe what Christ did is enough." When I do, God sees me just as He sees Jesus, for Jesus is my righteousness.

Furthermore, I'm not less righteous if I fail, or more righteous if I do good. In Christ, I am totally righteous, and when I sin as a believer in Christ, I'm not declared unrighteous. My actions may have been unrighteous, but the righteousness of God isn't based on my living up to a standard; my righteousness is in Christ. When I confess my sin, He forgives me and my righteousness remains intact. I'm not placed on probation for a few days or months when I fail.

So many people believe they are on probation when they sin and that they need to act better before God can forgive them. The Bible says I am forgiven by faith in Christ. I remain righteous all the while because my righteousness is in Christ; it is never uncertain or unstable. Therefore, I can rest assured in Christ and His work, letting Him bring forth the fruit of righteousness through me.

we are secure

Thus, we have a secure, confident standing before God in Christ. Romans 5:1–2 states, "Therefore, having been justified by faith, we have peace with God through our Lord Jesus Christ, through whom also we have obtained our introduction by faith into this grace in which we stand; and we exult in hope of the glory of God."

The word for *introduction* in Greek literally means "admission, access, or presentation," or "to bring into the presence of." It was used in reference to a person who would bring another person into the presence of a third person. The word was specifically used of someone who had secured for his friend an audience with a king. He would then bring his friend, properly attired, into the king's presence and favor. Jesus Christ has secured for us an audience with, and access to, the Father. He has properly attired us, wrapped us in His robe of righteousness, and brought us into the favor and the blessings of God. We have a standing that no one can take away. Jesus Christ is our admission, and through Him, we have total access and a firm standing before God.

When I was a kid, the professional baseball team in Seattle was called the Rainiers. When I went to a game, all I could afford to buy was a 50-cent bleacher ticket, but I would always sneak into the box seats. Often while sitting in those premium seats, the usher would come and ask to see my ticket. My face would get red and I would feel really foolish. Years later, a friend gave me a ticket to a Rainiers game, right behind home plate! I felt so good sitting in that seat, not worrying about an usher coming to bounce me.

There are so many Christians who wonder if it is all right to feel at peace; to believe they are forgiven when they are such a wretch. They ask, "Is it permissible to rest in Christ?" They're worried that the Lord is going to reject them, and Satan is there to accuse and condemn. They need to know their standing with God isn't uncertain or insecure for a moment.

Romans 5:2 exudes confidence: "… we have obtained our introduction by faith into this grace in which we stand." Paul doesn't say "in which we cower," or "in which we grovel around in self-defeat and unbelief." He says, "in which we *stand*." Through faith in Christ, you have a standing in God's grace, a position before God that no one can take away from you. Jesus speaks of our secure standing:

> My sheep hear My voice, and I know them, and they follow Me; and I give eternal life to them, and they will never perish; and no one will snatch them out of My

hand. My Father, who has given them to Me, is greater than all; and no one is able to snatch them out of the Father's hand.

John 10:27–30

in Christ

We have been placed in Christ who is at the right hand of the Father. Paul writes:

Even when we were dead in our transgressions, [God] made us alive together with Christ (by grace you have been saved), and raised us up with Him, and seated us with Him in the heavenly places in Christ Jesus.

Ephesians 2:5–6

That is your position. As you believe that and rest in your right standing with God in Christ, you will be amazed at the new perspective you will have on life. Your condition will begin to reflect that strong faith and life in Christ in whom you have been placed. The fruit of the righteousness of Christ will begin to be born more and more in you.

The following illustration emphasizes the importance of our standing and righteous position in Christ in the heavenly places. An officer in the American Flying Corps recalled, "I was out over the ocean alone, and I saw in the distance, coming rapidly toward me a storm that was blacker than midnight; the black inky clouds seemed to be coming on with lightning rapidity. I knew I could not reach shore ahead of the storm. I looked down to the ocean to see if I could go underneath it and perhaps alight on the sea, but the ocean was already boiling with fury. Knowing that the only thing to do was to rise above it, I turned my frail craft straight up toward the sky, and I let her mount 1,000, 2,000, 2,500, 3,000, 3,500 feet, and then the storm struck me.

"It was a hurricane and a cyclone and a typhoon all in one. The sky became as black as midnight. I never saw blackness like that. I could not see a thing. Rain came in torrents, the snow began to fly, the hail struck like bullets. I was 4,000 feet up in the air. I knew there was only one thing to do, and that was to keep on climbing. And so I climbed to 6,500 feet and then suddenly, I was swept out into sunlight and glory such as I never saw in this world before. The clouds were all below me, the sapphire sky was bending low above me in amazing splendor. It seemed the glory of another world. And I immediately began to repeat Scripture to myself, and, in the heavens above the clouds I worshipped God."[6]

The way out for that man was up, and so it is with us. The way out from self, from sin, from Satan's accusations and attacks, is up. God has placed us in the impregnable position of being in the heavenly places in Christ. As we abide and rest there, we will bear fruit.

4

righteousness by grace through faith

One of the most effective television commercials was the one done several years ago for Smith-Barney by the late British actor, John Houseman. He ended the commercial by saying, "We make money the old-fashioned way. We *eaaarn* it." The reason that commercial was so effective, aside from Mr. Houseman's accent and charm, was that it appealed to the basic human nature. We relish the thought that we can earn everything we need and want. Earning it, meriting it, deserving it, is truly the "old-fashioned" way, especially when it comes to atoning for our sins and gaining acceptability and approval.

When Adam sinned in the Garden, he tried to cover his sinfulness with a fig leaf that he had fashioned with his own effort, but it didn't work. Instead, God provided a covering for his sin with a garment of animal skin.

Years later, Adam's son Cain tried gaining approval just like his father, through the works of his own hands. He brought the produce of his garden to the Lord thinking that God was going to accept his offering. His brother Abel brought the best sheep of his flock and sacrificed it to the Lord. God had regard for Abel and his sacrifice, but God didn't have any regard for Cain or for his sacrifice. The reason for this is given to us in the New Testament: "By faith Abel offered to God a better sacrifice than Cain, through which he obtained the testimony that he was righteous" (Hebrews 11:4). Abel was trusting in God, but Cain was depending on his own works, the product of his hands. He was doing it the "old-fashioned" way, trying to earn it, trying to work for it. His efforts failed because God doesn't accept us on that basis.

In spite of these early failures, man has continued in the path of trying to earn God's approval through his own works. Why? Because it fits with our proud, independent, insecure nature. It is very humbling for us to admit that we are totally dependent on God when it comes to being acceptable and righteous, so we naturally tend to go on striving for approval. The fruit of this striving will be harmful until it finally hits us that we can't do it ourselves. Realizing that God has provided a secure, complete righteousness through Jesus Christ by simple faith brings peace and joy to the heart and mind.

by faith

God's way for us to gain righteousness and receive His blessings is not by works, but through faith. As Paul declares in Romans 4:1–9 (NASB):

> What then shall we say that Abraham, our forefather according to the flesh, has found? For if Abraham was justified by works, he has something to boast about; but not before God. For what does the Scripture say?

33

"And Abraham believed God, and it was reckoned to him as righteousness."

Now to the one who works, his wage is not reckoned as a favor, but as what is due. But to the one who does not work, but believes in Him who justifies the ungodly, his faith is reckoned as righteousness, just as David also speaks of the blessing upon the man to whom God reckons righteousness apart from works: "Blessed are those whose lawless deeds have been forgiven, and whose sins have been covered. Blessed is the man whose sin the Lord will not take into account."

Paul then adds, "For this reason it is by faith, that it might be in accordance with grace" (4:16).

There is a key question at the beginning of verse 3, "For what does the Scripture say?" This is the vital question if you want assurance, stability, security, peace and joy in your walk with Jesus Christ. What we think, or what others think about us, isn't important. Rather, what does Scripture say about your standing with God? It isn't important how we measure up or don't measure up to other people, or what they set as a standard. Neither is it important how you feel about yourself from moment to moment, or week to week. What is important is conforming our thoughts and feelings to what Scripture says about us. "To the one who does not work, but believes in Him who justifies [or who declares righteous] the ungodly, his faith is reckoned as righteousness" (Romans 4:5, NASB). If you have faith in Jesus Christ, God credits Christ's righteousness to your account.

spiritual giants?

Usually, we can see our own inability to be righteous with God, but at the same time we think, "If only I were more like Chuck Swindoll or Billy Graham. If I were just more like my pastor, then I could be more righteous with God." We assume these "spiritual giants" have a special, inherent righteousness; consequently, we're convinced we could never be as righteous as they are. The Jews probably felt the same way about their "spiritual giants," Abraham and David. Yet Romans chapter 4 makes it clear that Abraham and David's righteousness came from their faith in God, not their godly works. Today, we tell ourselves, "If only I was a good Christian." I hate that term, "good Christian." Every Christian is good. If your faith and trust is in Christ, you are righteous. Apart from Christ, there is no one who is good. As Romans 3:10 clearly states, "There is none righteous, not even one."

In Romans 4:3, Paul is quoting from Genesis 15:6 in the Old Testament: "For what does the Scripture say? 'And Abraham believed God, and it was reckoned to him as righteousness' " (NASB). Abraham wasn't always righteous; he wasn't born with a halo. The Bible tells us in Joshua 24:2 that Abraham was an idolater, just like his forefathers. But when God called him out of Ur of the Chaldees, Abraham responded in faith. God then gave him a promise concerning the Messiah. Abraham again believed God, and it was put on his account, "righteous." Abraham had nothing to boast about in his righteousness with God. He could have boasted if he had gained righteousness by his works, but he didn't. It was a gift from God which he received by believing.

There are no great men or women who have anything to boast about before God. Anything righteous or blessed about them comes from God. All of our boasting and glorying should be in God. There is nothing in us that is of any eternal value, nor good, nor righteous whatsoever apart from Jesus Christ. The Lord alone is worthy of our praise and glory.

Paul continues:

> Just as David also speaks of the blessing upon the man to whom God reckons righteousness apart from works: "Blessed are those whose lawless deeds have been forgiven, and whose sins have been covered. Blessed is the man whose sin the Lord will not take into account"
>
> *Romans 4:6–8, NASB*

This Old Testament quotation from Psalm 32:1–2 was written by David after he had been forgiven and God had covered his sin. When David committed adultery with Bathsheba and had her husband Uriah murdered, he covered up his sin. Yet, 2 Samuel 12:13 says that David confessed his sin to the Lord and the direct word of the Lord immediately followed: "The LORD also has taken away your sin; you shall not die." David was completely forgiven and his sin wasn't even put on his account. This wasn't because he was a godly man—David was an adulterer, a murderer, a liar, and a hypocrite—it was because of the Lord's mercy and grace.

David didn't do a thing to earn forgiveness; he put his faith in God and confessed his sin. Because he believed, God forgave his sin and put on his account, "righteous and blessed."

The same is true for all who place their faith in Christ. "To the one who does not work, but believes in Him who justifies [declares righteous] the ungodly, his faith is reckoned as righteousness" (Romans 4:5, NASB). The Lord doesn't justify godly people; there aren't any. Apart from His justification and His grace, there is no such thing as being godly, for according to Romans 3:11, "There is none who seeks for God"—not one. The qualifications for receiving God's righteousness are being ungodly, knowing you are ungodly, and admitting you need His righteousness because you realize you can't produce it in yourself. By faith, you receive forgiveness and He writes down on your account "righteous."

the wrong way

There are two ways to try to gain righteousness or acceptance with God. First, you can attempt to do it by your works, but you will constantly be striving to be good enough. On good days you will feel very righteous and want to let everyone know. This kind of righteousness is called self-righteousness and is a common problem among Christians.

On bad days you will feel unacceptable and condemned. Many people live with this kind of belief. They lament, "God's angry at me; He can't accept me because I'm such a terrible Christian."

If you are living this way, your righteousness will be inconsistent and not lasting, and you will never be fully certain of your acceptance. One day, you think you have just about made it, but the next day you slip. You will always be looking for formulas on how to be a good Christian, but you will never be fully certain. Even though you do a million different religious things, you will always be uncertain. And in the end it is all in vain anyway, for God says, "All our righteous deeds are like a filthy garment" (Isaiah 64:6).

a better way

There is a better way to gain righteousness than by your own works. It is by faith in Jesus Christ, God's provision for you. You can rest in the finished work of Christ on the cross and enter into His peace. Regardless of whether you have a good or a bad day, you are righteous in Christ Jesus because you believe in Him.

Your righteousness is an eternal gift through faith in Christ and failure doesn't change your standing with God. You aren't cast out from being a son or daughter because you have failed. In addition, you have assurance of acceptance before God in Christ. Jesus is totally acceptable to God. Therefore, if you are in the beloved Son, God's love is poured out on you in Christ.

Your relationship with Christ causes you to live in joy, peace, and fruitfulness. The righteousness that has been given to you as a gift begins to bear fruit and the security of Christ fills your heart and becomes a power source. In the end, you will be singing with Isaiah, "I will rejoice greatly in the LORD, my soul will exult in my God; for He has clothed me with garments of salvation, He has wrapped me with a robe of righteousness" (Isaiah 61:10).

It is your choice. Unbelief, insecurity, or pride causes us to work for our righteousness, but the Bible calls this "dead works." Dead works aren't going to make our conscience peaceful; they won't bring peace to our mind, heart or soul—that can only come from the blood of Jesus.

why faith?

Why is this righteousness of God given only by faith and not by any of our works? Paul provides the answer, "For this reason it is by faith, in order that it may be in accordance with grace" (Romans 4:16). God's grace is unmerited favor; you can't earn it, and you don't deserve it; you can only receive it as charity. Trying to work for righteousness and God's blessing is the wrong way. "Now to the one who works, his wage is not reckoned as a favor [literally, is not reckoned as grace], but as what is due" (Romans 4:4, NASB).

For example, when you get paid, you don't thank your boss for doing you a favor. Rather, he is obligated to pay you. Oftentimes, we Christians act as if God owes us something because of our spirituality or good works. There is a natural tendency for us to try to obligate God to bless us because of our acts of benevolence.

When we work to earn forgiveness or acceptance from God, we are seeking to obligate Him, because when we work for something we expect to receive payment. Your work obligates the person whom you are working for to pay you. You feel he owes you because you have done something good for him. Also, if you are working for someone, certainly before he hired you he was convinced that you could do the job. If you couldn't do the job, he wouldn't have hired you. When it comes to producing righteousness, God isn't hiring from the human race. We can't do the job and God doesn't want to pay us what our works deserve, because "the wages of sin is death" (Romans 6:23). He doesn't want to pay us that wage.

If you wonder why God isn't blessing you even though you have been very good, it is probably because you don't realize your desperate need for God. God doesn't bless on the basis of wages earned. "Who has first given to Him that it might be paid back to Him again?" (Romans 11:35). God won't be obligated or indebted to anyone. God doesn't owe us anything. Rather, we owe God something, but He knows we can't pay it. All He wants us to do is humbly cast ourselves in faith on Him and His provision. Then God's acceptance and blessing for us will come by grace as we receive it by faith.

> To the one who does not work, but believes in Him who justifies the ungodly, his faith is reckoned as righteousness. ... For this reason it is by faith, that it might be in accordance with grace.
>
> *Romans 4:5,16, NASB*

One of the most important lessons we need to learn is how to experience the glorious lifestyle of walking in God's grace. It's hard to receive grace graciously. Have you ever received a really nice present from someone and it wasn't even your birthday or Christmas? You hardly know what to say, because it was a love gift that you did nothing to deserve. God longs to pour out His grace and love, but we must humble ourselves and receive it in faith.

grace is undeserved

Grace is undeserved and unearned favor; it is God blessing us according to His loving nature. But not many people realize how much they need God; instead, they want to obligate Him. You won't get a thing from Him that way—He owes you nothing. Jesus' death on the cross for us is the righteous basis by which God can and does pour out His love on whomever He pleases. Because of what Jesus did, He can pour out His love without reservation. Our injustice and our sin has all been dealt with. Since God has no debts or obligations, He can and does pour out His grace on the least deserving who simply believe in Him. The Lord will bless and use them to confound the wise.

Grace can't act where there is deserving or ability. If there is ability, God's grace isn't needed. Many people don't bother to trust God's grace to get things done, because they are trusting their own plans and methods; they don't need the Spirit to work for them.

Grace, therefore, is uncaused by the recipient; its cause lies wholly in the Giver—God. We can do nothing for it but believe and receive. The reason lies with Him, not with us.

41

He loves us because He is love, not because we are lovely or lovable.

our position under grace

We are completely accepted in Christ who is our standing before God. Jesus Christ is our righteousness. When we fail, we assume we will have to wait two or three weeks to regain God's favor. But we aren't on probation to see if we are good enough for God's love. As to our former life without Christ, it doesn't exist before God. We died at the cross and Christ is now our life.

Our attitude under grace should be to allow God to love us, even though we are unworthy. He wants us to believe and receive His goodness each day, even in times of spiritual failure.

Also, we should refuse to make resolutions and vows; this is just trusting in the flesh. Maybe we commit the same sin for the twentieth time, so we come to God again and say, "Just one more chance, God, and I promise that I will witness five times." God knows we won't keep that promise either. Quit making vows; quit trusting in yourself. Give up on yourself and cast yourself on God. Apart from His Spirit, we won't make it, but through His Spirit, we can. There are times we make vows to try to give God a reason for blessing us. If we do that, we cut off God's grace. Don't try to deserve, just believe. By faith, expect God to bless you.

A person under God's grace isn't burdened for himself, but burdened for others. As you learn to live under grace, you will quit thinking about yourself and how bad you are. Instead, you will be thinking how good the Lord is and how you want to share Him with others.

principles to discover under grace

☐ To vow to be better is failing to see yourself dead and risen with Christ. You are seeing yourself apart from Christ and you don't want to do that.

☐ To be disappointed with yourself is to have believed in yourself. How many times have we said, or at least thought, "How could I have done that? I am so disappointed in myself." But God isn't shocked. He knows that when we are believing in ourselves, we will fail.

☐ To be discouraged is unbelief, because God has declared His blessing for us as fact. As we learn to live under grace, we will find unbelief is a big problem. This will be due to pride, insecurity, and various kinds of fear. Because the Lord has so much He wants to give us, we must not let discouragement rob us. Keep trusting and believing, and God's blessing will come as promised.

☐ To be proud is to be spiritually blind, for grace brings the utmost humility as we realize our absolute unworthiness. This is why grace is so hated by the proud, natural mind of man. The flesh has no place in grace, it can't earn it. We have a hard time receiving grace, because it puts our flesh back up on the cross.

43

We can't earn grace and the only place for our flesh is death. We need to thank God and glory in the cross on which we have been crucified with Christ.

❑ Lack of God's blessing is caused by unbelief, not failure of devotion. Many times, people assume God can't bless them because they haven't read the Bible or prayed enough. That isn't true; it is the other way around. If you let God bless you and let Him fill you with His grace, you will be so overwhelmed that you will want to seek Him more and more … and you will have the power and the strength to do it.

To preach devotion first and blessing second is to reverse God's order. It is actually preaching the Law rather than grace. The Law makes our blessing depend on our devotion. Many people believe if they are faithful in devotion and work hard, God will bless them. God doesn't approve if our works are trying to merit His grace. Rather, by faith we must simply receive His grace. This brings true devotion as a fruit. Now we are devoting ourselves to Him out of love. He has given us the strength through His grace to do what we could never do in our own power. God's grace is more than a passive principle, it is an active power and blessing in our lives.

grace: God's riches at Christ's expense

Does living under grace sound like the way you want to live? Absolutely! Does it make you want to go out and sin? No way! There are those who believe if you preach grace too much, people will just go out and sin, sin, sin. Truly receiving God's grace won't make you want to sin—instead, grace will always make you want to love and please God more. Now you have the power source: "Sin shall not have dominion over you, for you are not under law but under grace" (Romans 6:14, NKJV).

5

the roots of holiness

Within Christianity's recent past, there was a movement called the "Holiness Movement," which emphasized being holy before God. That emphasis was good, but they taught that a person could be holy by keeping certain rules of conduct. For example, women weren't to wear any makeup or any clothing that would show the knees or that was considered men's clothing. Men weren't to have long hair because it was effeminate, and they weren't to have beards because that was rebellious. In general, people weren't to go to theaters, dances, or bowling alleys where liquor was sold. No one was allowed to smoke, drink alcoholic beverages, or chew tobacco. By keeping these rules, you were considered holy.

Followers were also taught to do their best to crucify all their evil desires—they were to be diligent and intense in this. Some of them taught that you could actually attain sinless perfection through these means.

Again, there are those today emphasizing the importance of holiness unto the Lord. That is good because the Bible teaches us to be holy. The Lord says, "Be holy, for I am holy" (1 Peter 1:16, NKJV). Because holiness is so important, we need to know what it is and how God has prescribed that we attain it. We need to know God's true way according to the Scriptures. There is a pseudo-holiness that doesn't lead to true holiness, but really leads to a kind of self-righteousness, the root of which is the opposite of real holiness. Genuine holiness is found by getting to the root that produces holiness.

God isn't just an exterior designer, He is also an interior designer. Have you ever visited a house that was beautiful on the outside, but the inside was an old broken-down wreck? Jesus said to the Pharisees:

> Woe to you, scribes and Pharisees, hypocrites! For you clean the outside of the cup and of the dish, but inside they are full of robbery and self-indulgence. You blind Pharisee, first clean the inside of the cup and of the dish, so that the outside of it may become clean also.
>
> *Matthew 23:25–26*

Jesus doesn't merely want to make us look clean on the exterior, He wants to get to the root source of holiness in our lives.

unholy source is cut off

To provide this root source of holiness, Jesus had to cut out the root source of unholiness. He did this on the cross. On the cross, the unholy source of our old sin-controlled self, inherited from Adam, was cut off, and God condemned and crucified the entire sinful Adamic race. When God raised

Jesus from the dead, He began to create a new Christ-like human race. "If anyone is in Christ, he is a new creation; old things have passed away; behold, all things have become new" (2 Corinthians 5:17, NKJV).

Romans 5:17,19 (NASB) says:

> If by the transgression of the one [Adam's sin], death reigned through the one [Adam], much more those who receive the abundance of grace and of the gift of righteousness will reign in life through the One, Jesus Christ. ... For as through the one man's [Adam's] disobedience the many were made sinners, even so through the obedience of the One [Jesus Christ] the many will be made righteous.

Adam brought us into a state of sin, corruption, and condemnation, but Jesus undid the consequences of Adam's sin through His death on the cross and His resurrection. Through Jesus Christ, we can now experience an abundance of God's grace and righteousness.

As we live under grace there is a question we must answer that concerns holiness: "What shall we say then? Are we to continue in sin that grace may increase?" (Romans 6:1). In verse 20 of chapter 5, Paul had said, "Where sin increased, grace abounded all the more." So should we sin more living under grace to make grace increase? Verse 2 is Paul's clear, firm answer, "May it never be! How shall we who died to sin still live in it?" God's grace doesn't give us freedom to sin. Rather, it gives us freedom from sin and an entirely new source of power to be free.

Paul writes, "For sin shall not be master over you, for you are not under law but under grace" (Romans 6:14). This is a new source of life, forgiveness, and power. You are condemned by the Law, but you are given freedom and power through grace. Thus, grace doesn't lead us into greater sin, it actually frees us. This principle in found in verse 2: "How shall we who died to sin still live in it?"

sin is still alive

In order to understand what Paul is saying, we need to look at what he isn't saying, because people misunderstand the phrase "we have died to sin." First, he isn't saying that sin is dead in us. Sin isn't dead in us; sin is very much alive in us. As long as we are in these unredeemed bodies, sin is there. In Romans 7, Paul makes it clear that sin still dwells in us. Though we have died to sin we haven't reached a point of sinless perfection.

I have talked with people who believe in this. One time, I was playing with my children in the park when a young lady started chatting with me. She let me know she was a Christian and asked me if I still sinned. I said, "I would like to say I don't, but if I did I would be lying." She informed me that she hadn't sinned for about a year. I said, "It is really nice to meet you. I haven't met anyone like you for some time." In the course of our conversation, I shared with her verses such as 1 John 1:8 which states, "If we say that we have no sin, we are deceiving ourselves [no one else] and the truth is not in us." As I was sharing, she became really angry with me and said again, "I have not sinned in a year!" She couldn't see that she was sinfully furious with me.

The Bible doesn't say that our sinful nature has died. The sin in our fleshly bodies didn't die. But even though sin is very much alive, Christians have a new Christ-like nature. Our old selves were crucified and died with Christ so that our new selves could be dead to our sinful natures and alive to God. But sin is still there in us, and our sinful nature is still there.

crucify ourselves?

Many times, we are exhorted by well-meaning Christians to "crucify yourself." The Bible doesn't say that we are to crucify ourselves. Colossians 2:20–23 says:

> If you have died with Christ to the elementary principles of the world, why, as if you were living in the world, do you submit yourself to decrees, such as, "Do not handle, do not taste, do not touch!" (which all refer to things destined to perish with use)—in accordance with the commandments and teachings of men? These are matters which have, to be sure, the appearance of wisdom in self-made religion and self-abasement and severe treatment of the body, but are of no value against fleshly indulgence.

Trying to "crucify yourself" may look spiritual and self-denying, but it doesn't produce holiness at the root of your life. It is like cleaning up the outside but ignoring the inside, and it causes reliance on self instead of Christ.

J. Vernon McGee, the late pastor and popular radio Bible teacher, made the following comment: "I don't know about you, but I'm not able to crucify myself. The very interesting thing is that you can kill yourself in a variety of ways—by poison, with a gun, by jumping off a building—but you cannot crucify yourself. Maybe you can drive the nails into one hand on a cross, but how are you going to fasten the other hand to the cross? You cannot do it. How are you going to crucify yourself? You cannot do it. My young friend, you were crucified over nineteen hundred years ago when Christ died."[7]

identify in baptism

Or do you not know that all of us who have been baptized into Christ Jesus have been baptized into His death? Therefore we have been buried with Him through baptism into death, so that as Christ was raised from the dead through the glory of the Father, so we too might walk in newness of life. For if we have become united with Him in the likeness of His death, certainly we shall also be in the likeness of His resurrection.

Romans 6:3–5

One of our first acts of obedience as a young Christian is being baptized. Water baptism pictures our total identification and union with Christ in His death, burial, and resurrection. The key is found in verse 5, "If we have become united with Him in the likeness of His death, certainly we shall also be in the likeness of His resurrection." We have become united with Jesus Christ, placed in union with Him.

By God's doing, you are placed in Christ Jesus, who became to you righteousness and is now your source of holiness. The writer of Hebrews says, "For by one offering He has perfected for all time those who are sanctified" (Hebrews 10:14). Through the cross you have been separated unto God, because your old self has been cut off. Now the new self has been raised up in new life with Jesus Christ. When you put your faith in Jesus Christ, God unites you completely with Him in His death. As you understand the crucifixion of your old self with Christ and by faith consider it to be so, then you receive power from God to reject sin. You have the ability to say no to sin.

That brings us to the best news of all. The only root source for us to be holy is the risen Lord Jesus Christ—His life in you. As it says in Galatians 2:20, "I have been crucified with Christ; and it is no longer I who live, but Christ lives in me." It is the power of His life within us that enables us to be holy. We have become united with Him.

The word "united" literally means "grown together with." It is speaking of a living, vital union of growth. The picture is that of God grafting a branch into the stalk and roots of another tree, in order for the fruit of that branch to become good fruit. Paul says that we were cut off from what is by nature a wild olive tree and were grafted contrary to nature into a cultivated olive tree (Romans 11:24). We were cut off from the stalk of Adam, cut off from that old sinful self and grafted into the stalk of the second Adam, Jesus Christ.

no hope without Him

This further illustrates that there is no hope of holiness in our fleshly selves. But if the source of our holiness is the life of Jesus Christ and His power, there is no way that we can fail to be more holy. The key to becoming more and more holy is given by Jesus:

Abide in Me, and I in you. As the branch cannot bear fruit of itself unless it abides in the vine, so neither can you unless you abide in Me. I am the vine, you are the branches; he who abides in Me and I in him, he bears much fruit, for apart from Me you can do nothing.

John 15:4–5

The secret of holiness is depending on Christ and receiving the power and strength from Him to overcome. He is the source of our holiness.

Romans 6:6 gives us insight on how we have died with Christ:

Knowing this, that our old self was crucified with Him, in order that our body of sin might be done away with, so that we would no longer be slaves to sin: for he who has died is freed from sin.

In this verse, Paul explains what it means to be dead to sin. He states, "Knowing this, that our old self was crucified …" Our old self is all that we were from Adam—that old, natural, selfish, unregenerate person. The word "old" means old in the sense of being used, worn out, ready for the scrap pile. It couldn't produce anything good.

My first tape cassette player was an old portable model. I loved that thing, taking it wherever I went. I used it for years, but I never cleaned it or did anything to maintain it. After a while it didn't play tapes, it ate them—every single one! It got to the point where I hated it. Then one day, it was stolen out of my car. I was so happy. I was rejoicing!

That cassette player represents our old self—decayed, corrupted, destructive and useless. Not only did Jesus die for our sins to provide forgiveness, but through the powerful instrument of death, He has provided the means whereby we can have a new life. The old self was crucified with Him. It is as Paul said, "But may it never be that I would boast, except in the cross of our Lord Jesus Christ, through which the world has been crucified to me, and I to the world" (Galatians 6:14).

disconnected from the power

Romans 6:6 goes on to say, "our old self was crucified with Him, in order that our body of sin might be done away with." Our "body of sin" is our unredeemed body that still has the principle of sin dwelling in it. But this verse says our old self was crucified and our body of sin has been done away with. The Greek meaning doesn't imply that our body of sin has been done away with in the sense that it is no longer there or that it is destroyed. It is there, but it has been rendered entirely idle. Your sinful flesh has been made powerless if you believe that you died with Christ and have risen to a new life with Him.

Let me give you an example. When I was 13 years old, my older brother was crazy about cars. I enjoyed watching him fix up his old jalopies. He had this real nice metallic orange '57 Chevy that he had shined all up. Unbelievably, he asked me one sunny day, "Wayne, do you want to go down to the beach with me in my Chevy?" As we were headed down the main drag, he put it into first gear and took off as fast as he could. Then, as he was doing a power shift into second, he revved the engine and jammed it into gear. I was expecting some real "second gear scratch," but instead, all I heard was the roar of the engine.

There we were sitting in the middle of the street—he had blown the transmission! We were stopped dead with the engine roaring at 8,000 RPMs, but we weren't going anywhere. The transmission was blown, so the car's movement was disconnected from the transmission; we had been unplugged.

Through death with Jesus Christ, your old self has been crucified. As a result, you have been unplugged from that sinful flesh. Your body of sin has been put out of business, rendered inoperative. There are times when the temptation to sin is there, but you need to consider yourself to be dead to sin. By faith, you need to say, "No, I died with Christ. I am now a new creature with Christ Jesus. I can't do that." Because you have been disconnected, you have an entirely new source of power that gives you the freedom to say no.

Romans 6:6 also says, "for he who has died is freed from sin." The Greek word for "freed from sin" is literally "justified from sin." Not justified in the sense of being declared righteous from the guilt of sin, but justified from the power of sin. God knows that sin still dwells in us, but we don't need to fear it, because through Christ's death we now have power over sin. We don't need to be intimidated by its presence within us.

When my fleshly engine is roaring at 8,000 RPMs and I want to sin, I am naturally intimidated. I think I don't have any choice but to give into it. That isn't true because you are justified through your death with Christ. Yes, the presence of sin is there, but you don't have to give into it. You have died with Christ and have risen in His new life. We are united to Him in His death. You don't have to give into sin because you now have a new nature. You are free, you have a choice.

Christ is also alive within us. "Now if we have died with Christ, we believe that we shall also live with Him, knowing that Christ, having been raised from the dead, is never to die again; death no longer is master over Him. For the death that He died, He died to sin once for all; but the life that He lives, He lives to God" (Romans 6:8–10).

Christianity isn't only considering yourself dead all the time or dying on the cross all the time. It is also considering yourself alive with Jesus in a glorious new life. Jesus said, "If any man will come after me, let him deny himself, and take up his cross, and follow me. For whosoever will save his life shall lose it: and whosoever will lose his life for my sake shall find it" (Matthew 16:24–25, KJV). If you refuse to take up the cross with Christ you can't experience His life. The death of Christ is the entrance into the life of Christ; His death is the door. When you take up your cross and lose your life, you find his resurrection life. The cross is that instrument through which we can have the door opened for us into His resurrection life.

victory over sin

The resurrection life we share with Him is a life that gives us victory over sin. It is because of sin that Jesus died. Our sin killed Jesus Christ, but once He bore that sin, it didn't effect Him anymore. Now that He has risen and is seated at the right hand of the Father, sin has no more bearing on Jesus Christ whatsoever.

That is Jesus, but what about you and me? Ephesians 2: 6 says that you have been raised up with Christ and seated with Him in the heavenly places in Christ Jesus. You are now with Him. Even as sin doesn't bother Him, so it doesn't need to bother you. But you must rely on Him, receive His power, and abide in the heavenly places. The resurrection life is a life lived towards God. Before you were a Christian, you were dead to God and alive to sin. Now, it has been switched around and you are dead to sin, but alive to God. You have that life to keep you free from the power of sin.

Romans 6:11–13 tells us how we can experience death to sin and life toward Christ everyday: "Even so consider yourselves to be dead to sin, but alive to God in Christ Jesus. Therefore do not let sin reign in your mortal body so that you obey its lusts, and do not go on presenting the members of your body to sin as instruments of unrighteousness; but present yourselves to God as those alive from the dead, and your members as instruments of righteousness to God."

There are steps you must take in order to apply these truths and live in that source of holiness. First, you must by faith consider what God has declared to be true for you. You must "consider yourselves to be dead to sin, but alive to God in Christ Jesus" (Romans 6:11). The word *consider* is an accounting word. It means "to reckon, to put on your account, or to count it to be so." You have to believe what God has declared as a fact. Even though you may not feel like you are dead to sin, as you trust what God has said, you are given the power of the cross to say no. You are free because faith has received that power of the cross. Your faith in God's promise will squelch the horrendous temptation or sin that has been attacking you.

While Hudson Taylor was a missionary in China, he discovered what he called a "spiritual secret." Through simple faith in God, he was united with Jesus Christ and His resurrection life. He wrote:

All the time I felt assured that there was in Christ all I needed, but the practical question was—how to get it *out*. I knew full well that there was in the root, the stem, abundant fatness, but how to get it into my puny little branch was the question.

As gradually light dawned, I saw that faith was the only requisite—was the hand to lay hold of His fullness and make it mine. But I had not this faith. I strove for faith, but it would not come; I tried to exercise it, but in vain.

Seeing more and more the wondrous supply of

grace laid up in Jesus, the fullness of our precious Savior, my guilt and helplessness seemed to increase. Sins committed appeared but as trifles compared with the sin of unbelief which was their cause, which could not or would not take God at His word, but rather made Him a liar! Unbelief was, I felt, *the* damning sin of the world; yet I indulged in it. I prayed for faith, but it came not. What was I to do?

When my agony of soul was at its height, a sentence in a letter was used to remove the scales from my eyes, and the Spirit of God revealed to me the truth of our *oneness with Jesus* as I had never known before; but how to get faith strengthened? Not by striving after faith, but by resting on the Faithful One.' As I read, I saw it all! Ah, *there* is rest! I thought. I have striven in vain to rest in Him. I'll strive no more. For has not *He* promised to abide with *me*—never to leave me, never to fail me?[8]

It is a matter of resting in the facts, believing you are united with Christ, and considering that to *be so*.

don't let sin reign

The second step is not letting sin reign. Paul exhorts, "Do not let sin reign in your mortal body so that you obey its lusts" (Romans 6:12). By faith consider God's Word to be true, and say no. You have a choice: Say no to sin when it knocks. Don't let it reign. This verse is in the present tense, so it means stop letting sin reign; keep saying no.

Miles Stanford said, "In reckoning, our attitude becomes one of a firm stand against self, cost what it may. *The price of birth is His death for us; the price of growth is our death with Him.* ... This is the heart-attitude we, as believers, need today. Many of us unwillingly reckon on the crucifixion of the old man, only to draw back from the Cross when we feel the bite of the nails. It takes a real *hatred* of the old life, coupled with a deep *hunger* for the new, to be able to glory in the Cross that crucifies."[9] We have to be firm even though it hurts ... the cross hurts. Say no, and apply that truth.

"And do not go on presenting the members of your body to sin as instruments of unrighteousness" (Romans 6:13). The word *present* is literally, "put near." Don't put the members of your body near to sin. The following story illustrates this point. A little girl fell out of bed one night and began to cry. Her mother rushed into her bedroom, picked her up, put her in bed and asked, "Honey, why did you fall out of bed?" She answered, "I think I stayed too close to the place where I got in." And that's the reason a great many of us fall.

If it is so simple, why do we fall into sin? It is because we are still too close to sin. We are trying to remain Christians and Christ-like, yet we stay as close to sin as we can. Quit it. Don't place your members near sin. Rather, present yourself to God, get as close to God as you possibly can. That is the key, because He is the source of our lives.

In Romans 6:13, the word used for *instruments* is literally "weapons." We are in spiritual warfare. The kingdom of sin and Satan is fighting against the kingdom of God and righteousness. Let your members be allied with God in the fight. Don't let your members be allied with the enemy; present your body to God for His use and service. One main key to walking free from sin is to be so busy fighting *for* the Lord that you don't have an opportunity to fight *against* the Lord. Be so busy serving the Lord that you don't have time to sin against Him.

Holiness is a result of our union with Christ in His death and His resurrection life. Therefore, count yourself to be dead to sin and alive to God, presenting yourself alive to God moment by moment.

Let me give you a personal example. This may sound funny, but one of the hardest times for me in struggling with the sins of jealousy and malice is when I a mowing the lawn. Because lawn mowing requires no mental effort, I find my thoughts and attitudes wandering into the gutter of selfish ambition. As a pastor, I begin to mentally compare myself and my church with other pastors and their churches, and I sometimes become jealous. I begin thinking malicious thoughts about them to relieve my jealousy. You didn't think pastors could be so evil-hearted, did you?

Before long, the Holy Spirit convicts my heart, and as I mow the lawn I am grieved over my wrong attitudes. Immediately, I ask for God's forgiveness, and again become very thankful for the cross. In faith, I thank God that Jesus' cross has crucified that old selfish, jealous Wayne. I then begin to reject and say no to thoughts of malice and envy. Instead, I start praying for God to prosper those pastors and churches. I begin to rejoice in their effectiveness for God's kingdom. By this time, the lawn is looking good, and so is my heart.

6

winning the war within

Once my children and I were watching a Mickey Mouse cartoon on television featuring Mickey's dog, Pluto. Pluto found himself in a terrible dilemma—a kitten had come into the Mickey Mouse household and displaced him. Obviously, Pluto didn't like that cat. One day, the kitty fell into the well outside Mickey's house and was drowning. This put Pluto in a real predicament. Should he save the cat or let her drown? A little devil-Pluto appeared on Pluto's left shoulder saying, "Let that good-for-nothing, fat little cat die. She deserves it." But then, on the right shoulder there was a little angelic-Pluto saying, "Pluto, that poor little cat needs you desperately. Don't let her die, save her!" You can imagine the terrible turmoil. Pluto was being tugged back and forth ... it was an inner civil war.

Paul gives us the classic passage on this inner struggle:

For that which I am doing, I do not understand; for I am not practicing what I would like to do, but I am doing the very thing I hate. But if I do the very thing I do not wish to do, I agree with the Law, confessing that it is good. So now, no longer am I the one doing it, but sin which indwells me. For I know that nothing good dwells in me, that is, in my flesh; for the wishing is present in me, but the doing of the good is not. For the good that I wish, I do not do; but I practice the very evil that I do not wish. But if I am doing the very thing I do not wish, I am no longer the one doing it, but sin which dwells in me.

I find then the principle that evil is present in me, the one who wishes to do good. For I joyfully concur with the law of God in the inner man, but I see a different law in the members of my body, waging war against the law of my mind, and making me a prisoner of the law of sin which is in my members. Wretched man that I am! Who will set me free from the body of this death?

Romans 7:15–24, NASB

Does that sound like your autobiography? Could you have written those words? Oftentimes, we want so desperately to do the right thing, to do good, and yet we are defeated again and again. There is a power of sin which seems to defeat us every time.

two natures

This struggle takes place because we have two natures—a redeemed spirit in an unredeemed body. We have only a partially renewed mind. In my redeemed spirit and in my renewed mind, "I joyfully concur with the law of God in the inner man" (Romans 7:22). But in my flesh, the sinful nature that dwells in my unredeemed body, "I see a different law in the members of my body, waging war against the law of my mind and making me a prisoner of the law of sin which is in my members" (7:23). This can make for a fierce warfare between the flesh and the spirit. The word translated "waging war" literally means "attacking against each other." It is a tug-of-war and your mind is the rope. Like Pluto, you have your little devil-self and your angelic-self fighting back and forth; it is a huge tug-of-war. Pluto fortunately chose to save the kitten and became a hero. Ours isn't as simple a choice as a Disney cartoon.

There are two tendencies almost all Christians succumb to that actually increase our struggle. First, we rely on the willpower of our redeemed spirit, our new self, in order to do good and live righteously. Second, we try in our own strength to live up to God's righteous standards. These may sound good, but you soon find out that both of them will only increase the struggle and make the defeat even greater. Defeat isn't necessarily bad, depending on what you do with it.

We think that we can rely on the willpower of our new nature to do good and to live righteously. Paul tried to live that way and found it didn't work. He tells us what happened:

> That which I am doing, I do not understand; for I am not practicing what I would like to do, but I am doing the very thing I hate. … For the good that I wish, I do not do; but I practice the very evil that I do not wish.
>
> *Romans 7:15,19, NASB*

His new nature wanted to do the right thing, it was willing to do it, but every time he found himself failing, doing the very opposite of what he would like to do. Paul then discovered, "The wishing is present in me, but the doing of the good is not" (7:18, NASB). In other words, as a person who has a new nature in Christ, the desire is present in you, but the doing of the good is not.

A question arises: Why was the doing of good not in Paul when he was saved and had a new nature, a redeemed spirit? There are two reasons. First, because he not only had a new nature in him, he also had a sinful nature. Even as a Christian, while your old self was crucified with Christ, the sinful nature is still there. That sin in your flesh is still right there. Paul discovered, "I find then the principle that evil is present in me, the one who wishes to do good." There was a law of sin in his members. Second, the new nature Christ gives us doesn't overthrow our power to choose. Often, we still choose to follow our old nature.

The human race was originally created perfect, but is now infested with sin because God created us with the capacity of choice—free will. Sin is abusing that choice and choosing against God.

we don't have the power

We can't overcome sin by our own nature. The willpower of our new nature is not enough to overcome sin and live righteously. Our sinful flesh is too cunning. As you put your trust in your new nature, the flesh will use the goodness of your new nature to cause you to fall into sin. Consider this statement from William Law, "Your humility will help you to pride; your charity to others will give you nourishment to your own self-love, and as your prayers increase so will the opinion of your own sanctity."[10]

Putting confidence in our new nature, and not in Christ, can lead us to sin. We are to put our trust and confidence in God alone. One minute we are like wonderful Dr. Jekyll, the next minute like the hideous Mr. Hyde. Paul writes, "For the wishing is present in me, but the doing of the good is not." This shows the folly of appealing to your own will to live righteously. We may be willing, but we need to have the source of power in order to walk in the Spirit. Elsewhere Paul writes, "For it is God who is at work in you, both to will and to work for His good pleasure" (Philippians 2:13).

I grew up in a church where the pastor would call people to come forward and make a decision. Sometimes when he couldn't get unsaved people to respond (because they usually weren't there), he would get the saved people to respond. He would appeal to us, "If you need to be right with God, and if you want to live righteously before Him, come down and recommit your life to Christ." I held the record for recommitments—52 times! I was recommitting again and again and again. My problem wasn't unwillingness, it was that no one ever taught me how to walk in the Spirit. I had the new nature, but I hadn't learned how to continually tap into the power source of God's Holy Spirit.

the burden of production

We also have a tendency to try as hard as we can to live up to God's righteous and holy standards, but this leads to certain defeat. Since the struggle is with ourselves, whatever keeps us dependent on our strength, wisdom, love, patience, virtue or anything other than God, will make the struggle worse. Any form of law principle as the basis for your relationship makes you dependent on yourself. It puts the burden of producing fruit on you, and you can only fail apart from God.

This was the weakness of the Law. Paul writes, "For what the Law could not do, weak as it was through the flesh …" (Romans 8:3). The Law of God was never weak or faulty, the faultiness is with our sinful flesh. The Law of God is faithful to reveal to us the sinfulness of our deeds, making us that much more sinful. For example, if I tell my son, "Don't eat those cookies that Mom made," he is going to hang around those cookies because it is natural to his fleshly nature. On the other hand, if I don't say anything and put the cookies where he can't see them, it is a different story.

Paul says:

So then, the Law is holy, and the commandment is holy and righteous and good. Therefore did that which is good become a cause of death for me? May it never be! Rather it was sin, in order that it might be shown to be sin by effecting my death through that which is good, so that through the commandment sin would become utterly sinful.

Romans 7:12–13

God wants His standards to reveal our sinfulness so that we despair of ourselves, and realize that we can't live up to His standards by our own power. We have to place our faith in Jesus Christ. This was the purpose of the Law.

Paul wrote to the Galatians:

Is the Law then contrary to the promises of God? May it never be! For if a law had been given which was able to impart life, then righteousness would indeed have been based on law.

Galatians 3:21

If law could give you life and power to overcome sin, then a law-based relationship with God would be great. But all the law says is, "Do this, and if you don't you are dead." That doesn't give you any power, it brings condemnation. Paul continues:

But the Scripture has shut up everyone under sin, so that the promise by faith in Jesus Christ might be given to those who believe. But before faith came, we were kept in custody under the law, being shut up to the faith which was later to be revealed. Therefore the Law has become our tutor to lead us to Christ, so that we may be justified by faith. But now that faith has come, we are no longer under a tutor.

For you are all sons of God through faith in Christ Jesus. For all of you who were baptized into Christ have clothed yourselves with Christ.

Galatians 3:22–27

The purpose of the Law is to get you to despair of yourself and put your trust in Jesus Christ. Once you put your trust in Christ then you don't need the tutor anymore. If you are attempting to live up to the Law or religious standards in order to be pleasing to God, you are only going to fail, because it puts the burden of production back on you.

This is where Paul found himself; his big sin was covetousness. He couldn't overcome coveting, and of course the Law, in the tenth commandment, says, "Thou shalt not covet." This was his particular weakness. Through Jesus Christ he realized that the Law wasn't merely an outward command, it was also regulating his inward desires. Jesus said, "If you look on a woman to lust, you have committed adultery in your heart," and "If you hate your brother, you are guilty of murder." It isn't merely a matter of keeping the outward regulation. Once Paul understood that God's Law is more than an outward regulation—that it is a spiritual regulation—he realized how he had failed. Therefore he says:

> For we know that the Law is spiritual, but I am of flesh, sold into bondage to sin. … Wretched man that I am! Who will set me free from the body of this death?
>
> *Romans 7:14, 24*

learning from failure

This is the lesson that God wants to bring to us in our civil war struggle. He wants to teach us what Paul learned, "I know that nothing good dwells in me, that is, in my flesh" (Romans

69

7:18). We need to accept the fact that nothing good dwells within ourselves. Because we aren't convinced of our depravity, we don't rely upon the all-sufficient goodness of Jesus Christ. We continue to trust in ourselves, and consequently we continue to fail. The struggle goes on and on.

God lets us struggle. The struggle isn't bad, because it is to lead us to the place of total defeat where we will call upon Jesus and quit relying upon ourselves. This is what happened with Paul. He reached the point where he said, "Wretched man that I am! Who will set me free?" Paul had been a very self-confident man, therefore God had to bring him to this point of total failure.

God has to bring many of us to this same point, not because He likes to see us fail, but He has to let us fail as long as we are continuing to rely on ourselves. God knows it is harmful to let us succeed by trusting our own nature; thus He lets us fail. However, failure isn't the worst thing that can happen to you. When we fail we must say with Paul, "Wretched man that I am! Who will set me free?" That is the first step in our victory. Paul was no longer looking to himself, he was looking to an outside source. That is exactly where God wanted him. Paul proclaims, "Thanks be to God through Jesus Christ our Lord!" (Romans 7:25a). He has given me Jesus as my source with the empowering Holy Spirit flowing in and through me.

Paul also says:

Or do you not know, brethren (for I am speaking to those who know the law), that the law has jurisdiction over a person as long as he lives? ... Therefore, my brethren, you also were made to die to the Law through the body of Christ, so that you might be joined to another, to Him who was raised from the dead, in order that we might bear fruit for God.

Romans 7:1, 4–6

Paul is stating an obvious, common-sense fact: The law has jurisdiction over a person as long as he lives, but if he is dead he doesn't have to keep the law. If you are dead, you don't have to observe the speed limit or pay taxes. He then applies this truth, "Therefore, my brethren, you also were made to die to the law through the body of Christ. ..." He is referring to the death of Christ.

This brings us back to Romans 6:6 where it says our old self was crucified with Christ, so that our body of sin could be put out of business. In Romans chapter 6 we learn that we died with Christ, that we might know we are dead to sin. Romans chapter 7 tells us that we died with Christ, so we could realize we are dead to having to live up to the Law to please God. We are now released from the Law. When Jesus died, we died; the Law no longer has any legal claim on us.

We have a completely new basis of relationship with God. "You are not under law but under grace" (Romans 6:14). "For the Law was given through Moses; grace and truth were realized through Jesus Christ" (John 1:17).

This new relationship can be understood by the example of the marriage union. "Therefore, my brethren, you also were made to die to the Law through the body of Christ, so that you might be joined to another, to Him who was raised from the dead, in order that we might bear fruit for God" (Romans 7:4). You have been spiritually joined with Christ; "But the one who joins himself to the Lord is one spirit with Him" (1 Corinthians 6:17). In 1 Corinthians 15, Jesus is called a "life-giving spirit." Whereas the Law has no power to give you life or victory over sin, the life-giving spirit of Jesus Christ has that power as He fills you with His Holy Spirit.

God's love is unconditional

Our relationship with God is based on His unconditional love. As a husband, I don't go around my house tacking up little rules for my wife to keep. I don't say, "Honey, you have to do this, this, this, this, and this." I tried that, but it didn't work. No, it is a love relationship—not based on rules, but based on her desire to serve and love me. My love for her feeds that desire. I fall so far short of Jesus Christ, but He has a perfect, unconditional love for me, and as He fills my heart with that love I want to respond. His life and Spirit give me the power to respond.

Many times, people are looking for a set of rules to follow in order to become "good Christians." They will come to me and say, "If you are a Christian, can you still drink a glass of wine? How about two glasses? Three?" Or, "If you are a Christian, do you have to go to church? How many times a week? A year?" We like little sets of rules and laws. It is as if we are asking, "How much do I have to do to still be a Christian?

Where are the loopholes?" But Christianity isn't that kind of relationship; it is a love relationship, a living union.

When I'm asked to make rules, I respond, "Receive Jesus Christ and be filled with His Spirit, then love Him with all your heart, soul, strength and mind, and do whatever you want." That takes care of it; that is what the Lord desires. You are only going to be fully joined in love with Christ if you realize that He alone can carry you; you can't do it by your own power, you can't do it by yourself—it has to be Him. From that point on, you put all your trust in His strength.

Paul then says:

> While we were in the flesh, the sinful passions, which were aroused by the Law, were at work in the members of our body to bear fruit for death. But now we have been released from the Law, having died to that by which we were bound, so that we serve in newness of the Spirit and not in oldness of the letter.

Romans 7:5–6

Our service to God is an entirely new way of service. It isn't out of obligation or our own fleshly striving and energy; it is out of love and the power of God's Spirit.

Romans chapter 7 is only half of God's message, the negative half. But we must learn from chapter 7 to get to chapter 8, for no one goes straight from Romans chapter 6 to Romans chapter 8. There is a great struggle that we go through, and go back to, from time to time. As we learn these lessons more and more, we will learn how to walk in the power of His Spirit, instead of ourselves.

7

living in the power of the Holy Spirit

When I was a young boy, I loved to squish bugs and worms on the pavement. But no matter how hard I tried, I never was able to step on a butterfly. For one thing, they are hard to catch, and when you are little, they fly out of your reach easily. On a few occasions, I did manage to catch one, but have you ever tried to throw a butterfly onto the ground and step on it? They're like a yo-yo, they just don't stay down.

Satan is a mean, hateful adversary who loves to smash God's children in the dirt if he possibly can. He will hurt and ruin them. If we are groveling along like worms in the dust of self and the flesh, we are practically asking the devil to step on us and hurt us. Instead, we must take the wings of the Spirit that are rightfully ours and abide in heavenly places in Christ Jesus. Then no matter what our condition, Satan can't get to us, step on us or hurt us.

There are three keys to living in the power of the Holy Spirit. First, believe at all times that you are in Christ Jesus. Second, set your mind on the Spirit. Third, die to the flesh and live by the Spirit of God. In this chapter, we will be looking at the first key.

believe you are in Christ Jesus

Paul writes to the Romans:

> There is therefore now no condemnation for those who are in Christ Jesus. For the law of the Spirit of life in Christ Jesus has set you free from the law of sin and death. For what the Law could not do, weak as it was through the flesh, God did: sending His own Son in the likeness of sinful flesh and as an offering for sin, He condemned sin in the flesh, in order that the requirement of the Law might be fulfilled in us, who do not walk according to the flesh, but according to the Spirit.

> *Romans 8:1–4, NASB*

The word "therefore" in verse 1 takes us back to all that we have learned in the previous chapters. When you see the word "therefore" in the Scripture, you should always say, "What is it there for?" It always points back to something that was previously said and then draws a conclusion based on that which was said. In this case, it points back to the "facts of life" that we have learned so far:

1. Because of faith in Jesus Christ, we are right with God and completely secure. Romans 4:5 says, "To the one who does not work, but believes in Him who justifies the ungodly, his faith is credited as righteousness."

2. Our relationship with God in Christ is based on God's grace, not our works. We learned that "For this

reason it is by faith, in order that it may be in accordance with grace" (4:16). Grace is God's undeserved favor. "For sin shall not be master over you, for you are not under law, but under grace" (6:14).

3.   Our old self died with Christ on the cross to sin and to the Law. "Knowing this, that our old self was crucified with Him, in order that our body of sin might be done away with, that we should no longer be slaves to sin" (6:6). And Romans 7:4 says, "Therefore, my brethren, you also were made to die to the Law through the body of Christ." Thus, our old self died.

4.   Our new self has been united with the risen Lord Jesus who is our source of life. He alone frees us from our sinful flesh. Romans 6:5, says, "If we have become united with Him in the likeness of His death, certainly we shall also be in the likeness of His resurrection."

Paul cried out, "Wretched man that I am! Who will set me free from the body of this death? Thanks be to God through Jesus Christ our Lord!" (7:24–25). We are freed by being united with the risen Christ, who is our source of life.

Paul points back to those facts, but the bottom line truth is that we are *in* Christ Jesus. And so, "Therefore there is now no condemnation for those who are *in* Christ Jesus" (8:1, italics added). First Corinthians 1:30 says, "By His doing you are *in* Christ Jesus, who became to us wisdom from God, and righteousness and sanctification" (italics added).

The phrase "in Christ Jesus" is probably the Bible's most important description of Christians. Paul uses "in Christ

Jesus" over 85 times in his letters to describe our position. "In Christ Jesus" identifies you and me as being in the position of absolute safety and life. You are in Christ Jesus. Therefore, in faith determine never to see yourself outside of or apart from Jesus Christ, because He said, "Apart from Me you can do nothing" (John 15:5).

"If any man is in Christ, he is a new creature; the old things passed away, behold, new things have come" (2 Corinthians 5:17, NASB). When we are in Christ Jesus we aren't our old self. Romans 8:9 says, "However, you are not in the flesh but in the Spirit, if indeed the Spirit of God dwells in you. But if anyone does not have the Spirit of Christ, he does not belong to Him."

All genuine believers have the Spirit of God. The Apostle John wrote, "Whoever confesses that Jesus is the Son of God, God abides in him" (1 John 4:15). If you confess Jesus as the Son of God, as your Savior and Lord, then God abides in you. "By this we know that we abide in Him and He in us, because He has given us of His Spirit" (1 John 4:13). If you are in Christ Jesus, you are not in the flesh, you are in the Spirit.

There are many benefits found in realizing that you are in Him. Miles Stanford, in his book, *The Principle of Position*, wrote:

> All spiritual life and growth is based upon the principle of position. It can be summed up in one word: source.
>
> *Our position*, the source of our Christian life, is perfect. It is eternally established in the Father's

presence. When we received the Lord Jesus as our personal Savior, the Holy Spirit caused us to be born into Him. He created us in the position that was established through His work at Calvary. 'Therefore if any man be in Christ, he is a new creature [creation]' (2 Cor. 5:17). This is the eternal position in which every believer has been placed, whether he is aware of it or not. The Christian who comes to see his position in the Lord Jesus begins to experience the benefit of all that he is in Him. His daily state is developed from the source of his eternal standing.

Our condition is what we are in our Christian walk, in which we develop from infancy to maturity. Although our position remains immutable, our condition is variable. Through the exercise of faith, our eternal position (source) affects our daily condition, but in no way does our condition affect that heavenly position.

When we concentrate upon our condition, we are not living by faith but by feelings and appearances. The inevitable result is that we become increasingly self-conscious and self-centered. Our prime responsibility is to pay attention to the Lord Jesus, to rest (abide) in Him as our position. There will then be growth, and He will be more and more manifested in our condition. "But we all, with open face beholding as in a glass the glory of the Lord, are changed into the same image from glory to glory, even as by the spirit of the Lord" (2 Cor. 3:18).

If the believer does not know of his position in the Lord Jesus, and how to abide in Him as his very life, there will be but one result. He will struggle in his un-Christlike condition rather than rest in his Christ-centered position.

In most cases, a believer is more aware of his condition than of his position. This is the reason for so much failure and stagnation. If we are to grow and become fruitful, our faith must be anchored in the finished work of our position—in Christ. There is no basis for faith in our changeable, unfinished condition.

Scriptural, fact-centered faith in the Lord Jesus as our position before the Father is the one means of experiencing that finished work in the growth of our daily condition.

Every Christian has been positioned forever in the risen Lord by spiritual birth. But only the believer who knows, grows. It is faith in the facts of our position that gives us the daily benefits of growth in our condition. If the believer is not clearly aware of the specific truths of the Word, he cannot exercise the necessary faith for growth and service. He can only seek his resources in the realm of self.

We take our position, not by attempting to get into it, but simply by seeing that we are already positioned in the Lord Jesus. We abide in Him by resting in the fact. We have been in this risen position ever since our new birth. As we come to realize this truth and to "stand in our standing" in Him, we begin to experience the daily benefits of our life that is hid with Christ in God. Our attitude becomes, "I see my position in the Lord Jesus, and I abide there; I rest in Him, not only as my Savior, but as my life." Faith in our position will bring growth in our condition.[11]

It is important to realize that you are always in Jesus Christ. No matter your day-to-day, moment-by-moment condition, feelings, or experiences—you are in Him.

A major benefit of our being in Christ is that, "There is therefore now no condemnation for those who are in Christ Jesus." Before we can enter fully into the new life that God has for us, we need to know that we have been released from the condemnation of the old life. Condemnation prevents us from changing. Condemnation says, "You are wretched and you will never change. There is no hope for you. You are condemned in this state."

we are free

Condemnation boxes you in, but Jesus releases you from the box of condemnation. He grants forgiveness and cleansing, and then gives you new life to change and to be a new person. When someone assesses you negatively by saying, "You are this way," that really hinders you from changing. Jesus doesn't do that. Many people act as if God is ready and waiting to condemn, looking for them to step out of line. However, the opposite is true: "God did not send His Son into the world to condemn the world, but that the world through Him might be saved" (John 3:17, NKJV). Jesus didn't come to condemn us, but to save us.

Romans 8:3 (NASB) tells us why there is no condemnation for those who are in Christ Jesus:

> For what the Law could not do, weak as it was through the flesh, God did: sending His own Son in the likeness of sinful flesh and as an offering for sin, He condemned sin in the flesh.

Jesus took all of our condemnation. All of it! For all our sins past, present and future, the condemnation of God against sin was, and is, complete in the death of Jesus Christ for us. He is the God-man who bore the wrath of the Father in our place.

For the believer, his judgment day, as far as God's condemnation, is past. When Jesus said, "It is finished," that meant the end of Judgment Day for those who would believe in Jesus Christ. If you are in Christ, you need never feel that God is condemning you any more than He is condemning Christ, because you are in Christ Jesus. That frees us and makes us not want to sin. It frees me to want to be all that God wants me to be, to be all that I can be because of Jesus.

> Much more then, having now been justified by His blood, we shall be saved from the wrath of God through Him. For if while we were enemies, we were reconciled to God through the death of His Son, much more, having been reconciled, we shall be saved by His life.

Romans 5:9–10, NASB

I'm free to enter into that salvation and all the benefits of it, to be a new person.

God has set up absolute laws or principles to govern His universe—both physical laws and spiritual laws. For example, in the physical realm we have the law of gravity, which is a force of attraction keeping us connected to the ground rather than floating off into space. A person may not be conscious of these laws, but he is still under them. Most people don't even think about the law of gravity, but it is exerted upon them at all times. You can't negate these laws. If you try to negate these laws, you will only become more conscious of them. A doubter might say, "I don't believe in the law of gravity and I'm going to show you that the law of gravity isn't in effect. I'm going to go up to the top of a fifty-story building and jump off to prove to you that there is no law of gravity." This man will only become more conscious of the law of gravity when he hits the ground.

The only way to negate one of these laws is to counteract it with a higher law. With the law of gravity, we have the laws of aerodynamics. If we get into an airplane, it will use aerodynamic forces to counteract the law of gravity and actually supersede that law. So aerodynamic forces can free us from the natural restrictions of gravity. The law of gravity is still working, but a higher law has superseded it. This is demonstrated in my illustration of trying to step on a butterfly—I would throw the butterfly down and attempt to step on it, but its ability to fly allowed it to keep fluttering above the ground.

spiritual laws

As in the physical realm, God has set up certain laws in the spiritual realm. There are certain principles that are in effect here on earth. Romans 8:2 explains, "For the law of the Spirit of life in Christ Jesus has set you free from the law of sin and of death" (NASB).

What is "the law of sin and death" in regard to humanity? In Romans 3:23 we learned "all have sinned and fall short of the glory of God." Then Romans 6:23 added, "The wages of sin is death." In Romans 7:23 Paul writes, "I see a different law in the members of my body, waging war against the law of my mind, and making me a prisoner of the law of sin which is in my members." The law of sin and death is that we all sin, and this sin produces death. Sin also makes us prisoners. This is the law of sin and death that all humanity is under.

Anyone who sincerely tries to negate the law of sin and death only becomes more conscious of it. The harder you try not to sin and to live up to God's Law, the more conscious you become of your sinfulness. This is why self-help techniques, as far as trying to free ourselves from sin, are worthless. We only rearrange our sin. Or, if we take the positive mental attitude courses, we merely have more of a positive mental attitude about our sins. We are shifting the sin around, but not freeing ourselves from it at all.

The only way to be free from sin, to negate its power, is to put into effect a higher law. "For the law of the Spirit of life in Christ Jesus has set you free from the law of sin and death." By living in the life, power and direction of the Holy Spirit, we are free from the law of sin and death. The law of sin and death is still in effect, but it doesn't affect us if we are living in the Spirit, if we are living in the law of the Spirit of Life in Christ Jesus.

a life-giving Spirit

The Spirit of life in Christ Jesus is none other than the Holy Spirit of God Himself. It is the Holy Spirit who keeps us in Jesus Christ. He is the powerful one who changes our heart and empowers us in both our desires and our will to be free from sin. As Philippians 2:13 says, "It is God who is at work in you, both to will and to work for His good pleasure." Hence, the Spirit of life in Christ Jesus is the only effective antidote to the law of sin.

The secret for believers is to keep in close, spiritual touch with Jesus. Paul wrote to the Corinthians, "The last Adam became a life-giving spirit" (1 Corinthians 15:45). It says in John 3:34, "He gives the Spirit without measure." He wants there to be a constant flow.

The principle of life isn't the "storage-supply principle," like filling your car with gas once a week, though some Christians live their lives that way. The only consciousness of God or Jesus Christ they seem to exercise is on Sunday. The principle that we are to live by is the "contact principle." It is like the electric-powered buses in Seattle that have rods hooked up to wires which are connected to a power source. As long as the bus keeps its connection, it is receiving the power. If the rod is disconnected, the power is there, but the bus isn't receiving it.

The main power source for us comes through our faith in Jesus Christ; we need to recognize we are in Christ Jesus at all times. Our state, condition, situation, or feelings don't matter. We need to say, "Lord, I submit to You in this state. You know my condition, You know the situation. I yield to You in this setting, and I receive from You by faith. I am in Christ Jesus and I receive my rightful supply from You."

We don't have inherent power, even as Christians. We must remain in constant receptivity to Jesus through faith and obedience. As we do, His Spirit's life and power will gradually, and yet continually, transform us to become more like Him. This is a law for those who are in Christ Jesus. Living in the law of the Spirit of life in Christ Jesus will give you more freedom, but not freedom to sin. God's Holy Spirit at work within you won't fail to free you increasingly from sin, and make you more and more like Christ. Be patient and trust Him—it will happen. It's as certain as God's Word. It is the "law of the Spirit of life in Christ Jesus" for every true believer.

8

bearing, not manufacturing fruit

Like many, I enjoy fruit; in fact, I have a real weakness for it. I love going over to people's houses where they have bowls of fruit on the table. If I'm hungry, I'll ask for a piece, like a banana or an apple. If I'm extremely hungry, I'll just sneak one, and confess my sin later! I remember visiting a home once and there on the table was a big bowl of the most beautiful, luscious fruit I'd ever seen. It was so delicious looking, like a still life picture an artist would paint—so I decided to take one. I reached down, grabbed an apple, and just as I was ready to take a big bite, I realized it was plastic! All the fruit was fake—it had completely fooled me! Now, I don't have a problem with displaying plastic fruit, but somehow manufactured fruit doesn't taste quite the same as real fruit. Have you ever tasted plastic? No nutritional value whatsoever!

In Romans 8:2–4 (NASB) we observe the difference between fruit manufactured by ourselves, versus fruit that is brought forth by the power of God's Spirit in our lives:

> For the law of the Spirit of life in Christ Jesus has set you free from the law of sin and of death. For what the

Law could not do, weak as it was through the flesh, God did: sending His own Son in the likeness of sinful flesh and as an offering for sin, He condemned sin in the flesh, in order that the requirement of the Law might be fulfilled in us, who do not walk according to the flesh, but according to the Spirit.

Let's refer back to my fruit illustration. There's a huge difference between manufacturing plastic fruit and growing real fruit. For example, plastic apples have no meaningful relationship with an apple tree, other than being a lifeless copy of the real thing. You don't need an apple tree to manufacture a plastic apple. On the other hand, to bring forth real apples that are nutritious and tasty, an apple tree is absolutely essential, because real apples only come by being grown on apple trees. It's the life flow of the apple tree that produces the fruit of those delicious apples. In other words, luscious apples are the fruit of a relationship between a tree and its branches.

bearing good fruit

The same is true of a fruit-bearing Christian. Genuine fruit of the Spirit is the result of a relationship between us and Jesus Christ. The Lord is looking for fruit that is not manufactured by ourselves, but is brought forth by the Spirit of Jesus Christ in our lives. As verse 2 states, "For the law of the Spirit of life in Christ Jesus has set you free from the law of sin and of death." God's way of bearing good fruit in our lives is not by commanding us to produce it. He is not saying, "Bring forth good fruit now! Be good! Be holy!" The Old Covenant sought to tell us, "Do this! Do that!" but we were not able to, because we in ourselves can't produce good fruit. The weakness of the Law, according to verse 3, was the flesh. So God sent His Son and His Holy Spirit to do in us what we in ourselves could never do—bring forth wonderful, spiritual, righteous fruit.

How is it brought forth? Through a relationship. God doesn't work through an assembly line, as much of religion tries to make you believe. When you personally trust Jesus Christ and receive Him into your life, the Bible says God places you in Christ and He becomes the source and the power of a new way of living.

disconnected from sin

We learn in Romans 6 that when you trust Christ, the cross applied to your life cuts off your connection to the tree of Adam—the sinful, self-centered you—and plants you into a new source of living. Romans 6:6–7 (NASB) says:

> Knowing this, that our old self was crucified with Him, that our body of sin might be done away with, that we should no longer be slaves to sin; for he who has died is freed from sin.

Even though that old, powerful, sinful drive remains in our bodies, the cross disconnects us from it. Romans 6:8 goes on to say, "Now if we have died with Christ, we believe that we shall also live with Him" (NASB). God connects us vitally to a whole new source, the power of the life of Jesus Christ through the Holy Spirit.

connected through Christ

There's a lot of talk these days about being "connected." You need to be "connected" with the true and living God through Jesus Christ. God places you in Him and connects you to the other branches, through what Romans 8:2 calls "the law of the Spirit of life in Christ Jesus," which is just a wonderful term for the Holy Spirit. Jesus taught us about the Holy Spirit in John chapters 14–16. Right in the middle of that teaching, He gave a great lesson on the vine and the branches. It seems like Jesus was changing the subject, but when you understand who the Holy Spirit is, you realize He wasn't changing the subject at all, He was really hitting the heart of the issue. He said:

> I am the true vine, and My Father is the vinedresser. …
> Abide in Me, and I in you. As the branch cannot bear
> fruit of itself, unless it abides in the vine, so neither can
> you, unless you abide in Me. … If you abide in Me,
> and My words abide in you … you will bear much
> fruit, … for apart from Me you can do nothing.

the Spirit of life in Christ Jesus

How do we abide? The "Spirit of life in Christ Jesus" pours into us His marvelous presence and power. Through relationship we are empowered to do what we cannot do in ourselves. The Holy Spirit is the life flow coming out from

Jesus. In those chapters in John, Jesus said the Holy Spirit proceeds from the Father and from the Son. So Jesus pours in the Spirit, and reverently speaking, you could say the Holy Spirit is the "sap" of the vine flowing out into the branches. His life comes into the branches and fruit is born.

How is that fruit born? Not by striving and straining to produce fruit. Have you ever walked among fruit trees? It's very quiet. You never hear a fruit tree grunting and straining to produce fruit. Instead, within the wonderful relationship between the tree and the branches, an exchange of life takes place. Fruit grows by the branch drawing life from the trunk and staying connected and submitted to the tree.

How do you abide in Christ? Simply by a close, daily fellowship with Him through faith and surrender. We walk by faith, because Jesus is invisible. But He's very real. By faith, you open your heart to His Spirit and His Word, you surrender, and the Spirit works. Abiding in Christ is the same as living in the Spirit—they're identical. It's not us who produce righteous fruit for God, it's His Spirit. What a relief! We are not under pressure to perform and produce.

Look at Romans 8:4: "… that the righteous requirement of the law might be fulfilled in us who do not walk according to the flesh but according the Spirit" (NKJV). Though we are no longer under the Old Covenant Law as a basis for our relationship with God, the righteousness that God was seeking in that covenant has not changed. God hasn't lowered His standards now that we're under grace. Rather, He's lifted us up so that the requirement can be fulfilled in us through the power of His Spirit to do what couldn't be done in our own strength, nor through demands or commands upon us. Now we can walk in the power of the Spirit instead of the flesh.

the law is spiritual

Romans 7:14 says, "For we know that the law is spiritual; but I am of the flesh, sold into slavery under sin" (NRSV). God's Law has always been spiritual, but the problem is, I'm not spiritual. I'm carnal and fleshly; I'm not naturally godly—none of us are. But now, having been given the Holy Spirit who supplies us with the power to follow that new nature, I can be spiritual. Not spiritual in the sense of "holier that thou," but spiritual in the sense of being godly and wanting to please God with my life. Not being religious, but being Christ-like. Through the power of His Spirit, I don't have to be dominated by my flesh. Instead, He can fulfill in me that spiritual, righteous requirement of the Law.

love is the requirement of the law

What is that requirement of the Law? Love. In Matthew 22: 36–40 (NKJV), a lawyer approached Jesus and asked:

> "Teacher, which is the great commandment in the law?" Jesus said to him, "You shall love the LORD your God with all your heart, with all your soul, and with all your mind." This is the first and great commandment. And the second is like it: "You shall love your neighbor as yourself." On these two commandments hang all the Law and the Prophets.

Paul said, "love therefore is the fulfillment of the law" (Romans 13:10, NASB). Love is the "bottom line." That is what God meant in the Ten Commandments when He said, "You shall not steal." If we love our neighbors, we're not going to take what is theirs, we're going to respect them and their property.

You see how love goes above and beyond the Law? God commanded, "Do not bear false witness." If you love someone, not only will you not lie to them, but you will tell them the truth in love. He also commanded, "Do not commit adultery," for when you love someone, you're not going to indulge yourself and exploit them for your own pleasure. Rather, love is going to see them as created by God, deserving of honor and respect.

Romans 5:5 tells us that the Holy Spirit pours out the love of God in our hearts. God knows the number one need in your life is to feel loved, cared about, secure, and valued. Knowing you're looking for love, He says, "I want to pour love into your heart by My Spirit." So often, we're looking for someone else to satisfy our need for love. We seek out relationships to get what we need. But another person can never completely satisfy us. The only way to fill that void is through a relationship with Jesus.

The Lord has shown me, through much failure and disappointment, to draw from Him. Then through the Holy Spirit, He pours His love into my heart and I'm satisfied. He meets the primary need in my life for love. Sometimes He uses other people. For example, in marriage He wants to use spouses to show His love one to another. Or He might use a friend, or a brother or sister. He wants to use people, but He first wants to show His love to you directly, because He is blessed when we come to Him and say, "I need You." He then can be to us what He has wanted to be all along.

empowered by His love

As God fills our lives and satisfies our need for love, what happens? We can now be givers instead of takers. Because God is meeting our needs, we can begin meeting the needs of others. Instead of being self-seeking, we can be sensitive to others, because the Holy Spirit pours out the love of God in our hearts. In order for us to love, it is crucial to receive the love of God, moment by moment, day by day. Remember, "We love, because He first loved us" (1 John 4:19).

Paul writes, "… that the righteous requirement of the law might be fulfilled in us …" (Romans 8:4, KJV). He says the Law "might *be* fulfilled," because we don't fulfill it. If you determine by your own will that you are going to love God with all your heart, soul, strength and mind, and love people like Christ loves you, then you are going to fail miserably. That is the highest standard a person could ever seek to attain. You can't attain it, but it can be fulfilled in you. You are passive, or more precisely, actively-passive. You are actively depending on the Holy Spirit, because you know you can't do it. Therefore, the requirement of the law is fulfilled in you. The fruit of the Spirit is love; it isn't the fruit of myself or my effort. We need to be drawing from Christ as the source of our life.

I learned this lesson when I was eighteen years old. I was working next to a young man who was the most self-absorbed, petty person I'd ever known—he was a pain. I remember one day I went into the bathroom just to get away from him. I was complaining, "Lord, I hate this job and I can't stand this guy. Please find me another job." All I really wanted to do was gripe, but suddenly I was having a conversation with the Lord as He spoke questions to my heart.

"Do you love him?"

"No, I don't."

"Didn't I say, 'Love your neighbor as yourself,' and even, 'Love your enemies'?"

"Yes, but You said that before this guy was born."

"Do you think I love him?"

"Yes, of course; You love everybody."

"If I empower you to love him, will you?"

"All right. But You need to give me the love, because I refuse to love him on my own."

Immediately, the Lord gave me a sense of understanding about where this fellow had come from and why he acted the way he did. Then, I sensed a love from God and honestly, from that point on, I had no problem accepting him, caring about him, and relating to him. It had a tremendous impact for the Lord upon his life. The Lord did it—I was shocked myself!

tap into the life flow

There's something very interesting about the life flow of trees. It flows through the roots and the trunk uphill, against the pull of gravity, out to fuel and nourish the branches that produce the fruit. In the same way, the life flow of the Holy Spirit flows against the natural tendencies of your flesh. Often, even towards those we love most, we react in a negative way, while God's Spirit wants to help us care for them.

Understanding this has helped me so much in my marriage and how I treat my children. I fail in this area, but He keeps bringing me back to this truth, "If you would have drawn close to Me at that moment, I would have produced a different response." The primary work of God is to make us into loving people. It's a big job that's accomplished though drawing life from the Lord and submitting to Him.

My very first car was an old Volkswagen Bug that had a reserve gas tank. When I was out of gas, I just flipped a switch and started drawing gas from this second tank. A non-Christian only has one tank—his own. But we as Christians have two tanks—our own and the Holy Spirit's. The problem with our tank is that it's about the size of an eyedropper! It doesn't go very far. For example, I can be patient "for a little while," or I think, "I'll be kind to him as long as he's kind to me." But the Lord's tank is infinite—a gigantic, universal-sized tank! Keep it switched on His tank instead of your own, or when you realize you've been running on your own tiny tank, switch back to being empowered by Him.

bear real fruit

Being empowered by the Spirit through a living relationship of faith and submission to Jesus is the key to bearing real fruit. If you want fake stuff, manufactured fruit will do. But it won't be that tasty, nutritious, wonderful fruit of love that Christ produces.

In conclusion, I would like to draw again from the writings of Miles Stanford:

> In the natural realm, the life that is already complete in the vine is increasingly supplied to the growing branches. The healthy condition of the branches is contingent on their abiding in their position in the vine. The branch is not only a product and living part of the vine, but that which is produced in the branch is also the fruit of the vine. Actually, the branch produces nothing, either for the vine, for others, or for itself. The vine, the positional source, has everything to do with the development and fruitfulness of all its branches. The chief responsibility of the branch is to rest just where it was born, to abide in its living position in its living source.

> As the believer rests in his position, the life of the Vine (the "fruit of the Spirit") is manifested in his condition—"love, joy, peace, patience, kindness, goodness, faithfulness, gentleness, self-control" (Gal. 5:22–23, NASB). The life of the Vine is the life of the branch.[12]

9

the battle for control of our lives

There was a boy in my sixth grade class whom I will probably never forget, though I would like to! There are two reasons why I will never forget him. First, he had a name that is hard to forget: Delbert Wypff. Second, he would beat me up almost every day. You tend to remember those who beat up on you.

Each time I fought with Delbert, I thought I was going to beat him, but he always slaughtered me. Strange as it may seem, because he beat me up so often, I began to feel close to him. I finally accepted that Delbert was always going to beat me up, so I made friends with him. He still picked on me, but I knew I couldn't do anything about it, so I took it. After several months of this routine, Delbert moved away. A few weeks later, I realized how good it felt to not get beat up anymore!

Many of us are like that with the flesh—we are getting beat up by it. At first we are self-confident that we can conquer the flesh. After a while, it conquers us so much that we accept its dominance as a familiar friend. We get used to it. However, the flesh, unlike my friend Delbert, isn't going to move away. It is that principle of sin still dwelling in us, and every time you move, it moves with you. God has given us a powerful Helper, the Holy Spirit, through whom we put to death the deeds of our flesh and enjoy lasting victory. The Holy Spirit can free us and give us victory over our own flesh.

As Christians, we need to understand at all times that we are in Christ; He is our position before God and the source of our spiritual life. As we believe in Him, see ourselves in Him, and draw from Him as the source of our lives, then we will experience that life-giving Spirit. Our condition will begin to reflect our position as we grow in our knowledge of Jesus.

other keys

We will now consider two more keys to living in the power of the Holy Spirit. The second and third keys can be found in Romans 8:5–13 (NKJV):

> For those who live according to the flesh set their minds on the things of the flesh, but those who live according to the Spirit, the things of the Spirit. For to be carnally minded is death, but to be spiritually minded is life and peace. Because the carnal mind is enmity against God; for it is not subject to the law of God, nor indeed can be. So then, those who are in the flesh cannot please God.

> But you are not in the flesh but in the Spirit, if indeed the Spirit of God dwells in you. Now if anyone does not have the Spirit of Christ, he is not His. And if

Christ is in you, the body is dead because of sin, but the Spirit is life because of righteousness. But if the Spirit of Him who raised Jesus from the dead dwells in you, He who raised Christ from the dead will also give life to your mortal bodies through His Spirit who dwells in you.

Therefore, brethren, we are debtors—not to the flesh, to live according to the flesh. For if you live according to the flesh you will die; but if by the Spirit you put to death the deeds of the body, you will live.

on things above

The second key to living in the power of the Spirit is to set your mind on the things of the Spirit and not on the things of the flesh.

The battle between the Spirit and the flesh for control of your life is fought primarily in your mind. The word translated "mind" in verses 5–7 includes both our thought life and our emotions. It is speaking about both our thoughts and our feelings. As Spirit-born Christians, though we are in the Spirit, it doesn't necessarily follow that we will walk according to the Spirit.

There are two prepositional phrases here. One is being "in the Spirit," and the other is walking according "to the Spirit." Paul writes, "But you are not in the flesh but in the Spirit, if indeed the Spirit of God dwells in you" (verse 9). If we have put our trust in Jesus Christ for salvation and received His Holy Spirit, the Bible says we are "in the Spirit."

The unsaved person is in the flesh and "those who are in the flesh cannot please God" (verse 8). A person who is unsaved, who doesn't have the Holy Spirit, cannot please God with his life. Though believers are in the Spirit, it is possible for them to continue to walk according to the flesh. The phrase, "according to the flesh," in verse 5 is from the Greek word *kata* meaning "down on the level of the flesh." Though you are in the Spirit, you can still walk down on the level of the flesh, because you still have that principle of sin dwelling in you.

Galatians 5:25 states, "If we live by the Spirit, let us also walk by the Spirit." Though Christians have the Holy Spirit, God doesn't take away freedom of choice. Since we have that principle of sin living in us, we still have the flesh to contend with. For us to walk by the Spirit, we must choose to set our minds on the things of the Spirit and not on the things of the flesh. The reason it is so important to walk by the Spirit and not by the flesh is found in Paul's admonition to the Galatians, "I say then: Walk in the Spirit, and you shall not fulfill the lust of the flesh" (Galatians 5:16, NKJV).

There is only one way to live a life free from following the desire of the flesh: Walk by the Spirit. We can't defeat our flesh by our flesh, nor can we defeat our flesh in our own power, or through our schemes or plans. It must be by the Spirit.

The realm in which we walk is determined by what fills our thoughts and feelings. What fills your mind during the day? Is your mind filled with anxieties and cares about the pressures of life? Maybe you're worried about the future or about something you did in the past. Or do you think about getting rich? Or maybe getting married ... or unmarried?

Do you have malicious thoughts about people like your boss, one of your fellow workers, someone in school, someone who has wronged you, or maybe even a good friend? Are you constantly plagued with anger and bitterness? Do covetous, lustful thoughts fill your mind?

Jesus said we are to love the Lord our God with all our mind [thoughts] and heart [feelings] (Matthew 22:37). The battle for control of our lives is fought in our hearts and minds. That is the battlefield. Whatever controls our thoughts and feelings is going to control our lives.

what is filling your heart?

Have you ever been driving with a cup of coffee or water in your hand when suddenly, you hit a big bump in the road? Usually, your drink spills out all over you! If it's coffee, which leaves a stain, you probably weren't too happy about it. You might even need to go home and change your clothes. But if it's only spilled water, that's not such a big deal, especially if it's a hot day.

Jesus said, "Out of the abundance of the heart the mouth speaks" (Matthew 12:34, NKJV). Whatever is filling your heart—meaning your thoughts and your feelings—that is what's going to come out. He went on to say in Matthew 15:19,20, "For out of the heart come evil thoughts, murder, adultery, sexual immorality, theft, false testimony, slander. These are what make a man 'unclean' " (NIV). It's not only our conversation that proceeds from out of our mouth, but our conduct actually comes from what's within our heart. We do what we've been thinking about. This makes it very critical that whatever fills our hearts is good and godly. In Matthew 12:35, Jesus said, "A good man out of the good treasure of his heart brings forth good things, and an evil man out of his evil treasure brings forth evil things" (NKJV).

So what fills our hearts and minds is what will spill out of our lives, especially when you go through the "bumps" of life. The stressful, difficult times have a way of pushing out whatever's been filling the inside. If it's sinful and selfish thoughts, they will spill out and defile you, much like spilled coffee leaves a stain. If you put coffee into a cup, water is not going to spill out. It's the same spiritually. If your mind has been set on carnal things, the living water of God's Spirit is not going to spill out and refresh you when you need it most.

king of the mountain

When I was a boy, I used to play a game called "King of the Mountain." We had this little dirt hill on our block and all the neighborhood kids would struggle with each other to get to the top. Once someone reached the top, it was hard to pull them off, because they had the position where they could throw challengers down. Often, our fleshly desires, passions, and thoughts seem almost impossible to pull down, to get out of our hearts and minds. They are continually defeating and plaguing us. Second Corinthians 10:3–5 (NKJV) says:

For though we walk in the flesh, we do not war

according to the flesh. For the weapons of our warfare are not carnal but mighty in God for pulling down strongholds, casting down arguments and every high thing that exalts itself against the knowledge of God, bringing every thought into captivity to the obedience of Christ.

God has given us divinely powerful weapons with which we can capture our thoughts and feelings. We don't have to allow our thoughts and feelings to control the direction of our lives, as if we are helpless pawns and they are a horrible dictator ruling over us. By the mighty Spirit of God, we must pick up the weapons God has given us and take charge of our thoughts and our feelings for His glory.

One mighty weapon is prayer in the name of Jesus. Paul wrote in Philippians 4:6,7, "Be anxious for nothing, but in everything by prayer and supplication [pouring out your needy heart in prayer, crying out to God] with thanksgiving let your requests be made known to God. And the peace of God, which surpasses all [understanding], will guard your hearts and your minds in Christ Jesus." If you find control of your thoughts and feelings slipping away through anxieties, worries, or temptations … pray. Luke 18:1 records that Jesus taught His followers to pray always and not lose heart. Then God's peace will stand watch over you like a garrison protecting you from harm.

blood of Christ

We must take advantage of spiritual weapons like the blood of Jesus Christ which cleanses our hearts and minds. In

Revelation 12:11 we read, "And they overcame him because of the blood of the Lamb." Whom did they overcome? The accuser of the brethren that was cast down. When Satan attacks you with temptation or with accusation, plead the blood of Jesus. Through His blood, your heart and mind will be cleansed, protected, and covered.

worship

Another weapon is worship. Worship isn't only a wonderful privilege, but it is also a mighty weapon that focuses us, keeping us protected and centered upon Jesus Christ. We find this in David's encounter with Goliath, the Philistine giant. Goliath said to David:

"Come to me, and I will give your flesh to the birds of the sky and the beasts of the field."

Then David said to the Philistine, "You come to me with a sword, a spear, and a javelin, but I come to you in the name of the LORD of hosts, the God of the armies of Israel, whom you have taunted. This day the LORD will deliver you up into my hands, and I will strike you down and remove your head from you. And I will give the dead bodies of the army of the Philistines this day to the birds of the sky and the wild beasts of the earth, that all the earth may know that there is a God in Israel, and that all this assembly may know that the LORD does not deliver by sword or by spear; for the battle is the LORD'S and He will give you into our hands."

the battle for control of our lives

Then it happened when the Philistine rose and came and drew near to meet David, that David ran quickly toward the battle line to meet the Philistine. And David put his hand into his bag and took from it a stone and slung it, and struck the Philistine on his forehead. And the stone sank into his forehead, so that he fell on his face to the ground.

1 Samuel 17:44–49

Though David was probably frightened, he started praising the Lord and declaring his trust in Him. God then conquered the enemy.

sword of the Spirit

One of the most powerful weapons we have available to us is the Sword of the Spirit: the Word of God. God's spoken Word created this world out of nothing. Likewise, that Word of God is holding together all of the mighty power in the universe. The Bible says:

The word of God is living and powerful, and sharper than any two-edged sword, piercing even to the division of soul and spirit, and of joints and marrow, and is a discerner of the thoughts and intents of the heart.

Hebrews 4:12, NKJV

We discern what is of the flesh, what is of the soul, and what is of the Spirit by the Word of God. It divides and judges. The Word of God is a sword whereby we can take those evil thoughts as prisoners of war.

Second Corinthians 10:5 says, We are destroying speculations and every lofty thing raised up against the knowledge of God, and we are taking every thought captive to the obedience of Christ." We can do this through the Word of God. It is important to memorize verses that relate to your particular area of fleshly weakness. You have to be armed and ready when that attack of temptation returns. David said, "Your word I have treasured in my heart, that I might not sin against You" (Psalm 119:11).

If you aren't ready with the Word, it is nobody's fault but your own. It only takes a little bit of time to actively prepare your mind and heart for the attacks that will come. And they will come, for Satan knows our weaknesses, and he is going to tempt us. But the Word of God is mighty and it can help us withstand the temptation.

Once we have the Word of God hidden in our hearts, then we must set our minds on those Scriptures and not on the fleshly temptation. The King James Version translates Romans 8:5, "For they that are after the flesh do mind the things of the flesh." In English, "mind" has two meanings. It means "our thoughts," but it also means "to obey."

I often tell my children, "Mind me." I'm saying obey me and my thoughts, not your own. The same is true for us. If we are to set our minds on the things of the Spirit, we must mind the Spirit, obey the Spirit, and obey the Word of God. We aren't going to be able to both disobey and walk in the

Spirit; our hearts and minds need to be filled with the Word, and then we must yield in obedience to it.

the things of the Spirit

What are the things of the Spirit that we should set our minds upon? Is it memorizing Scripture and thinking on verses all the time? Is it praying every second? Is it thinking only about God and not being able to think about working hard, or having fun, or being with our family and friends, or just relaxing? Some people believe those pursuits aren't spiritual, and that you always have to be thinking about God. But the Bible tells us, "Every good gift and every perfect gift is from above, and comes down from the Father of lights with whom there is no variation or shadow of turning" (James 1: 17, NKJV).

God has given us many good things, it is only the heart and mind of man that has perverted them and made them into idols. Our hearts need to be filled with wholesome things, relationships, and activities. As it says in Ephesians 4: 23, "Be renewed in the spirit of your mind." Instead of your thoughts being of selfish indulgence and selfish glory, your root attitude should be one of pure love toward God and others. Those are the things upon which the Spirit is wanting us to think.

Of course, a major part of that is God's Word, God Himself, and prayer. But there are other wholesome and wonderful things. Philippians 4:8 teaches, "Whatever is true, whatever is honorable, whatever is right, whatever is pure, whatever is lovely, whatever is of good repute, if there is any excellence and if anything worthy of praise, let your mind dwell on these things." These are the things of the Spirit of God; that is what He is going to lead us to think about. As we do, His mighty power and His weapons will keep us protected and victorious against the flesh and against the things of the flesh.

warfare

The consequences that result from what we let fill our minds are found in Romans 8:6: "For the mind set on the flesh is death, but the mind set on the Spirit is life and peace." There is a battle for our hearts and minds between the Spirit and the flesh. It is warfare and, as with any warfare, there is grave danger. We can either conquer or be conquered. The flesh and the Spirit are mutually exclusive, they can never peacefully coexist.

> So then, brethren, we are under obligation, not to the flesh, to live according to the flesh—for if you are living according to the flesh, you must die; but if by the Spirit you are putting to death the deeds of the body, you will live.
>
> *Romans 8:12–13*

Because they can't peacefully coexist, it is either kill or be killed.

tending your heart's garden

In the battle for our hearts and minds, we have two choices:

We can consistently utilize the spiritual weapons God has given us, or we can allow our carnal minds to dictate and dominate us. Paul told the Galatians:

> Do not be deceived, God is not mocked; for whatever a man sows, that he will also reap. For he who sows to his flesh will of the flesh reap corruption, but he who sows to the Spirit will of the Spirit reap everlasting life.
>
> *Galatians 6:7–8, NKJV*

In other words, it's all a matter of "agriculture." Your heart and mind are a garden that God has given you. How fruitful, fragrant, and beautiful your garden is depends on how you take care of it.

Some of us want a flower garden, but instead we plant wild oats, then pray for a crop failure! When those wild, carnal thoughts are allowed to stay, soon they take root, choking out the goodness of God's Word. You can't stop these thoughts from entering your mind, but you are responsible if they lodge there. Martin Luther once said, "You can't keep the birds from flying over your head, but you can keep them from building a nest in your hair."

I've noticed something about gardens: Weeds grow so much easier and bigger than flowers. You don't even need to plant weeds … they grow all by themselves. The same is true with our fallen flesh. You don't need to plant ungodly thoughts, they just come in on their own. Many times a day, use the weapons God gives to weed and water the garden of your mind and heart. Through the power of His Spirit, plant the wonderful flowers and fruitful seeds of the good things of God.

die to the flesh

Living according the Spirit is a "life and death" situation: We must die to our flesh and live through the Spirit. Suppose some enemy attacked my wife and children. Do you think I would sit there passively watching and say, "Isn't that a shame? That guy is killing my wife and kids. That's awful!" Would I do that? No! I would rise up and do whatever I had to do to prevent him from harming them—even if it meant killing him—because I am the protector of my family. They are precious to me.

But how much more precious is the life that God has placed within us. God has placed within us the very life of Jesus Christ through the Holy Spirit. The flesh will kill us, yet so often, we find Christians flirting with the flesh.

If you are living according to the flesh, you must die. The flesh is horribly deadly, and it brings death to our spiritual walk. I have witnessed more casualties to the flesh than I can count. They just subtly began to yield to the things of the flesh. Soon, they were living after the flesh and have fallen away from Jesus Christ. The flesh is a deadly enemy. I have seen many others living in a continual beaten-down state because of the flesh, and that isn't what God wants at all.

We don't owe the flesh anything. What did the flesh ever do for you except enslave you, hurt you, and deaden your spiritual life? And yet, we keep going back to it. We forget, like the children of Israel forgot what it was like in Egypt. All they could think about was the enticing foods they had left behind. They forgot that they had been beaten and enslaved. We forget. But then, when we taste again of the flesh we realize how deadly it really is. More and more, we shun it and turn to the Spirit.

We don't owe the flesh anything, but we owe our very souls to Jesus Christ. Therefore, we owe it to God to crucify the flesh, that we might live full lives in the Spirit. "But if by the Spirit you put to death the deeds of the body, you will live" (Romans 8:13, NKJV).

It is difficult to put to death the deeds of the flesh because it is our basic human nature. The flesh takes many forms: pride, self-will, self-righteousness, worldliness, and rebellious tendencies against God. When we let the Spirit crucify the flesh, it is going to hurt. It is painful, but it's worth it.

Dying to the flesh by the Spirit is the "trap door" to a glorious resurrection life filled with the Holy Spirit. That is why Samuel Rutherford wrote, "Christ's cross is the sweetest burden that ever I bore; it is such a burden as wings are to a bird, or sails to a ship, to carry me forward to my harbour."[13] When Jesus said, "Take up your cross and follow Me" (see Matthew 16:24), He was giving us that key to walking in the Spirit. At times, the Holy Spirit will lead us to die to our flesh. It will hurt, but it is a blessed pain, and it is something that goes on throughout your Christian walk.

The more you experience the cross, the more you will agree with Paul:

But God forbid that I should boast except in the cross of our Lord Jesus Christ, by whom the world has been crucified to me, and I to the world.

Galatians 6:14, NKJV

As we die to the flesh and are filled with the life of the Holy Spirit of God, we will be living in His power. In summary, remember to believe at all times that you are in Jesus Christ, set your mind on the things of the Spirit and not on the things of the flesh, and by the Spirit, die to the flesh and live filled with the Spirit's love. Those are the keys to living in the power of the Spirit.

10

pass the ball to Jesus

One night, I was watching sports highlights on television when they showed the exciting finish of a basketball game between the Seattle Supersonics and the San Antonio Spurs. It had come down to the end of the game, just a few seconds left, and the Spurs were behind by one point. With the game on the line, Shawn Kemp got the ball and tossed it in the basket from eighteen feet, winning the game for Seattle.

If you were on a basketball team, you would want to have a team member like Shawn because he is what is known as a "franchise" player: Athletes who make the team successful because they are winners; they will bring any team to the playoffs and to a victory because they are so great.

When I was in junior high, I played basketball. We had an incredible center on our team named Steve Hlastala who was 6'5". He was muscular and coordinated, a tremendous athlete. It was so fun being on his team because I played guard and I was only about five feet tall. I would dribble the ball down the court and get it to Steve. He would take the ball and shoot it over everyone's heads into the basket, scoring another couple of points. Steve loved having me on his team because he knew I wanted to win and I would always get the ball to him.

The only other team that had a big center was Monroe Junior High. Their center was tall, but skinny—like human spaghetti. He was a good player and he could block all of our shots except Steve's. He was also able to shoot over all of us and make it, except over Steve. So, when he came down the floor with the ball, I just got out of the way and let Steve take him. Steve was so much better and did such a good job guarding him, that the Monroe guy usually fumbled the ball. Then, I would grab it, dribble down the court, and make a lay-up.

on His team

This chapter is entitled "Pass the Ball to Jesus" because when you are on Jesus' team, when you are in Him and He is in you, you are more than a victor. Jesus is a franchise player in the game of life … He *is* the franchise. He can do anything and everything right; He knows everything about everything—how to meet your needs, how to solve your problems, and how to take care of any situation. He knows how to direct you to the right people and the right places. He knows what He is doing, and when you are with God, you are a victor.

Paul poses these questions, "What then shall we say to these things? If God is for us, who can be against us? He who did not spare His own Son, but delivered Him up for us all, how shall He not with Him freely give us all things?" (Romans 8:31–32, NKJV).

When Paul asks, "If God is for us, who can be against

us?" he isn't saying there is some question as to whether God is for His children. Throughout Romans, Paul has made it very clear that God is for us. A better translation would be, "Since God is for us, who can be against us?" Who is against us, who could possibly stand in the way of our victory? David said in Psalm 56:9, "This I know, because God is for me" (NKJV).

There are many things that I don't know. When tough times come and I have a great loss, or I am facing some terrible hardship, there is much that I don't understand. But one thing I do know, God is for me. Do you know that? Is that a confident assurance that you have in your life? God isn't out to get you. His goal isn't to take away your joy, to hurt you, to restrict or ruin your life. God is your Heavenly Father. I love to see my kids happy and I love to have fun with them. I don't like to chastise and discipline them, but I do so because they need it. My goal is for their good, because I love them. God causes all things, even those things that aren't from Him, to work together for good to those who love Him. He is Lord of all, including our enemies. He is in control of what they are allowed to do.

In Romans 8:32, Paul presents the proof that God is for us: "He who did not spare His own Son, but delivered Him over for us all, how will He not also with Him freely give us all things?" God allowed Jesus to die in order that we could know how much He loves us. "God demonstrates His own love toward us, in that while we were still sinners, Christ died for us" (Romans 5:8). What more could God do to convince us that He is for us?

Oftentimes, we assume that God isn't for us, but that is a wrong assumption. He didn't spare the grief and suffering of His Son, in order that He might bear our sorrows. He didn't spare His Son being beaten, scourged, and whipped with 39 lashes, in order that we might be healed. He didn't spare His Son's crushing wounds, so that we could be released from our sin, cleansed, forgiven, and restored. According to Isaiah 53: 10–11, the Lord was pleased to crush Him, in order that He might render Himself a guilt offering to justify us, to declare us righteous before Him.

Paul assures us, "He who did not spare His own Son, but delivered Him over for us all, how will He not with Him also freely give us all things?" (Romans 8:32). God has already given us Jesus Christ. Any further need you might have isn't that big in comparison. If God gave us so great a gift as His Son, then obviously He won't withhold from us anything that is good for our walk with Him. Along with the gift of His Son, He will "freely give us all things." The key is that you have to pass the ball to Jesus. Seek Him first and He will add all these other things. Pass the ball of your concerns to Jesus Christ. He knows what to do and has the power to meet your need. He is a master at everything.

The Lord is the one who can guard you from your enemies. If you try to stand up to Satan on your own, he will beat you every time. Let Jesus Christ guard, protect, and keep you. God is able to turn the tide on the enemy and use the same schemes against him. If God is for us, who is against us? Because God *is* for us, we can handle anyone and anything.

The devil is our enemy, so it is important that we have

some understanding about the schemes of the one "who is against us." As 2 Corinthians 2:11 states, "… lest Satan should take advantage of us; for we are not ignorant of his devices" (NKJV).

In the series of questions Paul asks in Romans 8:33–37 (NKJV), we learn something about the purposes of the devil in his attacks against us. We also learn something of the purposes of God in our struggles, hardships, and difficulties. In these questions, we see the progression of Satan's attacks:

> Who shall bring a charge against God's elect? It is God who justifies. Who is he who condemns? It is Christ who died, and furthermore is also risen, who is even at the right hand of God, who also makes intercession for us. Who shall separate us from the love of Christ? Shall tribulation, or distress, or persecution, or famine, or nakedness, or peril, or sword? As it is written: "For Your sake we are killed all day long; we are accounted as sheep for the slaughter." Yet in all these things we are more than conquerors through Him who loved us.

Here we find God's purpose for allowing adversities, as well as Satan's purpose in those same adversities. In this series of questions, we discover a progression: "Who is against us?" Satan. "Who will bring a charge against God's elect?" Satan. Revelation 12:10 calls Satan the accuser of the brethren "who accuses them before our God day and night." Satan loves to accuse and bring a charge against God's elect. This is an effective attack for him, because often his charges against us are true. He accuses us of some failure, some horrible deed— and he is right, we *did* do it. He attempts to get us to believe that we can't come to God and receive the love of Christ, because God is angry with us and doesn't want anything to do with us anymore. That is a lie!

Paul writes, "Who will bring a charge against God's elect? God is the one who justifies." Satan is always bringing a charge against us, but God already knows we have done wrong. He knew all the sins that we would commit throughout our lifetime before He ever saved us. Our sins haven't caught the Lord off guard. He saved us in order that He could free us from the harmful effects of sin. He not only forgives, He frees us from sin's power.

God justifies on the basis of the blood of Jesus Christ, "Being justified freely by His grace through the redemption that is in Christ Jesus" (Romans 3:24, NKJV). Jesus took the penalty for all our sins. Scripture shows us how we can overcome these accusations: "And they overcame him because of the blood of the Lamb ..." (Revelation 12:11). We don't appeal to God from the basis of our goodness or because we aren't "that bad." Yes, we *are* "that bad," but His sacrifice was sufficient.

satan's purpose

In Romans 8:34, Paul asks, "Who is the one who condemns?" Satan's purpose in his accusation is to condemn us, because he wishes to destroy our relationship with God. Our relationship with God is a walk of faith, not a walk of sight. There is nothing that will weaken our faith more quickly than a guilty conscience. If we are plagued with guilt and a sense of constant failure and worthlessness, we aren't going to be able to trust in God.

It is so important to keep our conscience clear. We can't keep violating our conscience and harming the delicate nature of our heart, and have a strong faith and strong walk with God. We can't do it. Put away the old self and all its sin, and put on the new self. Don't give the devil an opportunity. Satan condemns us because he wants to weaken our faith and destroy our relationship with God.

Satan has been foiled. "Who is the one who condemns? Christ Jesus is He who died, yes, rather who was raised, who is at the right hand of God, who also intercedes for us" (Romans 8:34). With His death, Jesus Christ took our condemnation, then He rose in demonstration of that fact. There is no condemnation in Him. God accepted His sacrifice and now Jesus is at the right hand of the Father, interceding for us, praying for us, and constantly advocating our position of "no condemnation" before the Father. As a matter of justice—because He is a just, righteous, and holy God—Jesus answers the charges brought against us. His blood, the Bible says, completely covers and cleanses us. We aren't condemned, but are righteous in Him. Therefore, Jesus lives to make intercession for us, so that He can eternally save us.

Thus, there is a big difference between condemnation and conviction. Condemnation comes from Satan and from our own insecure hearts, but conviction comes rightfully to us from the Holy Spirit. Both condemnation and conviction say, "You did wrong," but that is where the similarity ends.

Condemnation says, "You did wrong. You can't come to God and receive the love of Christ." Conviction says, "You did wrong. Come to God and receive forgiveness that you might again receive the love of Jesus Christ." Condemnation pushes you away from God, conviction draws you toward God. Condemnation says, "You are wrong and you are hopeless," conviction says, "You are wrong, but there is hope in Jesus Christ." That is a big difference.

If you are ever feeling pushed away from God or like you can't come to God, don't believe it. It is a lie. Romans 8:1 tells us, "Therefore there is now no condemnation for those who are in Christ Jesus." The Holy Spirit will touch your conscience and tell you, "Come to Christ for forgiveness, cleansing, and freedom." That is the Holy Spirit, drawing you and offering hope and renewal.

satan's ultimate goal

What is the ultimate goal of Satan's attacks? Paul asks, "Who will separate us from the love of Christ?" (v. 35). Satan's ultimate goal is to cut you off from the love of Christ, but he can't do it. Paul continues, not "angels, nor principalities … will be able to separate us from the love of God, which is in Christ Jesus our Lord" (Romans 8:38–39). Satan can't separate you from the love of Christ, and he knows that. But if he can make you think you are cut off from the love of Christ, then he can make your life unfruitful. That is Satan's desire. He wants to prevent you from receiving that resource you so badly and constantly need—the love of God. Hence, he seeks to block you from God's love through accusation, condemnation, and through other means.

> Shall tribulation, or distress, or persecution, or famine, or nakedness, or peril, or sword [separate us from the love of Christ]? As it is written: "For Your sake we are killed all day long; we are accounted as sheep for the slaughter."
>
> *Romans 8:35–36, NKJV*

Satan hates you. This is a genuine description of his estimate and goal for your life. To him, you are demon-fodder. He wants to slaughter you in every way he possibly can. Jesus said:

> The thief comes only to steal and kill and destroy; I came that they may have life, and have it abundantly.
>
> *John 10:10*

According to Romans 8:35, Satan has a purpose. Fortunately, God also has a purpose. The word translated, "tribulation or trial," is the Greek word *thlipsis,* meaning "pressure." Satan attacks by pressuring us with the circumstances of life. He uses those circumstances to beat us down and make us feel hopeless. But pressure isn't necessarily bad. Pressure will cause your tire to blow-out, but it also takes pressure to fill up your tires. Pressure will cause stew to boil over on the stove and onto the floor, but it also takes pressure to cook stew.

Satan's goal is to cause you to blow-out and boil over;

to lose your temper and get in the flesh. God's desire in tribulation is to fill you and to "cook" you; to build His character into your life. Paul says:

> We also exult in our tribulations, knowing that tribulation brings about perseverance; and perseverance, proven character; and proven character, hope; and hope does not disappoint, because the love of God has been poured out within our hearts.
>
> *Romans 5:3–5*

Pressure is the beginning of God pouring out His love in you and then through you. You persevere while you are being filled with the love of God. That is the process of God in tribulation. Satan wants to destroy you, but God wants to build your character and make you into a loving person.

distress

Then there is distress. The Greek word for distress can be literally translated, "a narrow, cramped place," meaning hemmed in with no apparent way of escape. Have you ever had claustrophobia? It is a scary feeling. When I was in my first year of junior high school, I was kind of a smart-aleck. One day, I was showing off and I allowed my friends to talk me into getting into my locker. As soon as I got in, they slammed the door and turned the lock. I went crazy! I started screaming and crying, which is not cool for a seventh grader. I was hemmed in and I was so scared.

Satan loves to use the distressing circumstances of life to

strike fear in our hearts. He tries to destroy us by convincing us God has left us. He plagues us with thoughts of horrible terror and fear.

But that can't separate us from the love of God. He sometimes allows us to be hemmed in like the children of Israel. It was God who led the Israelites out of Egypt and right up to the Red Sea. Before them was the Red Sea with Pharaoh dragging up the rear. God knew that was going to happen, but He didn't lead them there to destroy them, nor has He led you into your situation so that the enemy can destroy you. He has allowed you to get in that position to show you His power of deliverance and more of Himself than you have ever seen. In these times God is revealed to you in a very real way. No one wants to experience these times that the Lord often allows. Remember, Moses lifted up his staff, the Red Sea parted, and the children of Israel were delivered by the mighty power of God. The same will be true for you.

persecution

Finally, there is persecution. The Scriptures tells us, "All who desire to live godly in Christ Jesus will be persecuted" (2 Timothy 3:12). You will be made fun of, you may even have physical abuse for the sake of Christ. They persecuted Him, they will persecute us. But Jesus also said:

Blessed are [you], when men shall revile you, and persecute you, and shall say all manner of evil against you falsely, for my sake. Rejoice, and be exceeding glad:

123

for great is your reward in heaven: for so persecuted
they the prophets which were before you.

Matthew 5:11–12, KJV

How is it that when we are being persecuted we think we
have done something wrong? Don't think that. Don't think
God is against you. He is not. God is saying, "Blessed are
you, because in this situation, I want to comfort and minister
to you, and become more real to you." You are laying up
treasures in heaven that become greater through these trials.

In Romans 8:35, Paul goes on to mention famine,
nakedness, peril, and sword. The "sword" refers to death. He
is saying that even in death, the love of Christ isn't separated
from us. Death merely ushers us into the fullness of His love.
Paul knew about all these things, because he experienced
them all. Eventually, he was beheaded for the cause of Jesus
Christ. But his death was quick, and he has been in heaven
enjoying the love of Christ for 2,000 years. Do you think Paul
has thought at all about those terrible trials he experienced?
Death, the worst possible circumstance, only draws us that
much closer to Jesus Christ.

Paul continues, "But in all these things we overwhelmingly
conquer through Him who loved us" (Romans 8:37). We are
more than conquerors. The Greek literally says we are "super-
conquerors" through Him. Jesus is the franchise, the one to
whom you must pass the ball. When you are going through
tribulation, you have to rely on the power of the Lord. When
you are in distress, pass the ball of your concerns to God.
When you are experiencing hardship, give it to the Lord,

don't sit there and fret about it. The Lord knows you can't handle it; your frame and your psyche aren't meant to handle all that pressure. That is why He has given Himself to you.

plant your flag

Paul concludes, "For I am convinced that neither death, nor life, nor angels, nor principalities, nor things present, nor things to come, nor powers, nor height, nor depth, nor any other created thing, will be able to separate us from the love of God, which is in Christ Jesus our Lord" (Romans 8:38–39).

We have come within a few feet of the summit. When mountain climbers come to the summit of a previously unconquered mountain, they can hardly wait to take the flag of their team or country and make those final few feet to the summit. They are filled with authority and excitement as they plant that flag on the summit and say, "It is mine, I have conquered it." Here we are at the summit, at the conclusion of the "facts of life," and truly these are principles of life. We are at the summit of Christian living in these verses that tell us, "Nothing can separate you from the love of Christ."

Get out your flag of faith and realize that nothing can or will separate you from His love. Plant your flag, take Him at His Word. He says not even death can separate you. Death is but a transition to the ultimate things of God. There is a natural fear of the unknown, but we know what it holds. The Bible says that the sting of death is sin. If you die in your sin without Christ's forgiveness, it means eternal judgment. But Jesus took the sting out of death.

I have a brother-in-law who is scared stiff of bees. He is frightened because of their stingers. Jesus has taken away the stinger. For us death is a glorious transition. We don't want to die, but when the time comes we need not fear, for God's grace will be with us.

Neither can fallen angels, nor Satan, nor principalities, separate us. They are nothing compared to God. Neither "things present nor things to come" can separate us. No matter how difficult your present circumstances are—that financial stress, that breakup of a relationship, that legal problem you have, that sickness, or whatever it might be—they can't separate you from God's love. God wants to show us His love as we go through the tough times.

The "things to come" can't separate us, because God holds the future in His hands. His loving grace will be there at the appropriate time. "Nor powers." There is no power on earth as great as the love of God. "Nor height, nor depth." No ups and downs, highs and lows, nor any change you are going through, can separate you from the love of Christ. You may feel that it has, but it has not. To make certain you understand, Paul adds, "Nor any other created thing." He includes the whole world. Nothing can separate you from the love of God that is in Christ Jesus our Lord, because you are in Him and *nothing* can take you out of His hands.

God loves you as He loves Christ. That love is yours. All you have to do is receive it from Jesus. The great English poet and songwriter, Charles Wesley, said, "Jesus, Thou art all compassion. Pure, unbounded love Thou art. Stronger Thy love than death or hell, its riches are unsearchable."[14]

Our hope, our security, our joy, our peace, our assurance, our endurance, isn't in *our* love for Christ, but in *His* stubborn, steadfast love for us.

A beautiful sister of old, Mrs. Merrill E. Gates, wrote this in 1886:

> *Thy love to me; O Christ,*
>   *Thy love to me,*
> *Not mine to Thee, I plead,*
>   *Not mine to Thee.*
> *This is my comfort strong,*
>   *This is my joyful song,*
> *Thy love to me,*
>   *Thy love to me.*

My friend, firmly plant your flag of faith here, and Jesus' love for you will help you be victorious in your civil war within.

notes

[1] Maxwell, L.E. *Crowded to Christ* (Grand Rapids, MI: Wm. B. Eerdmans Publishing Company, 1950), p. 67.

[2] Ibid, p. 54.

[3] Bainton, Roland. *Here I Stand: a Life of Martin Luther*, pp. 49–50

[4] Hession, Roy. *Calvary Road* (London: Christian Literature Crusade, 1950), p. 84.

[5] McDowell, Helen, from "The Continual Burnt Offering." H. A. Ironside, Loizeaux Bros., 1941.

[6] Maxwell, L.E. in "Sunday School Times." *Crowded to Christ* (Grand Rapids, MI: Wm. B. Eerdmans Publishing Company, 1950), p. 30.

[7] McGee, J. Vernon. *Romans* Chapters 1–8 (Nashville, TN: Thomas Nelson, Inc., 1991), p. 106.

[8] Maxwell, L.E. *Crowded to Christ*, pp. 54–55.

[9] Stanford, Miles J. *The Complete Green Letters,* from The Reckoning That Counts (Grand Rapids, MI: Zondervan, 1983), pp. 217–218.

[10] Maxwell, L.E. *Crowded to Christ*, p. 66.

[11] Stanford, Miles J. *The Complete Green Letters,* from The Principle of Position, pp. 77–78, 81.

[12] Ibid, pp. 80–81.

[13] Maxwell, L.E. *Crowded to Christ* (Chicago, IL: Moody Press, 1976), p. 67.

[14] Wesley, Charles (1707–1788). *Love Divine, All Loves Excelling,* 1747.

about the author

WAYNE TAYLOR, the senior pastor of Calvary Fellowship in Seattle/Mountlake Terrace, Washington, is a stimulating and practical teacher who relates biblical truths to the needs of today. He is the featured speaker on the radio program *Consider Jesus* and the author of four books: *He Dwelt Among Us: A Daily Devotional Through the Gospel of John; Practical Christian Living* (a study of Romans chapters 12–13; *The Unsearchable Riches of Christ,* a 30-Day devotional from the book of Ephesians; and *The Civil War Within.* Wayne and his wife Cathy live in Seattle and have four children.